*BEFORE THERE WAS AN
AMERICA—NOSTRADAMUS
FORETOLD HER FUTURE.*

Renowned scholar David Ovason reveals how
Western history's most remarkable clairvoyant
predicted the most momentous events in the
development of the United States, including:

- The settlement of Jamestown
- The Declaration of Independence
- The founding of St. Louis
- The development of electricity
- The invention of manned flight
- The Apollo space program

and

- The terrorist attack on America and the
destruction of the World Trade Center

NOSTRADAMUS— PROPHECIES FOR AMERICA

Also by David Ovason

THE SECRET ARCHITECTURE OF OUR NATION'S CAPITAL
THE SECRETS OF NOSTRADAMUS

NOSTRADAMUS

PROPHECIES

for

AMERICA

DAVID OVASON

AVON BOOKS

An Imprint of HarperCollinsPublishers

AVON BOOKS
An Imprint of HarperCollins*Publishers*
10 East 53rd Street
New York, New York 10022-5299

First Avon Books paperback printing: November 2001

Avon Trademark Reg. U.S. Pat. Off. and in Other Countries, Marca
Registrada, Hecho en U.S.A.
HarperCollins ® is a registered trademark of HarperCollins Publishers
Inc.

Printed in the U.S.A.

10 9 8 7 6 5 4 3 2 1

Contents

●

NOSTRADAMUS

PROPHECIES

for

AMERICA

Introduction

•

Twelve verses, written in the 16th century, relating to the United States of America

It was the beginning of an event that will surely change the world.

At 8:45 A.M., on Tuesday, September 11, 2001, a hijacked Boeing 767, carrying 92 passengers and crew, and with 10,000 gallons of aviation fuel on board, crashed into the north tower of the World Trade Center, in Manhattan. The Boeing was traveling at 300 miles per hour.

It was the worst act of terrorism the world has ever seen, and the heavens seemed to reflect its horror. At that moment, the planet Mars was in the same degree as the lunar Dragon's Head. Further in space, the planetary destroyer, Pluto, was conjunct ("joined" or "united") with the violent star Rastaban, the yellow eye of the constellation Draconis.[1] The Arabic-speaking hijackers of the Boeing 767 would have called this star *Al Rās al Thu'bān*, the Head of the Dragon.

This obscure-seeming astrology almost helps us get our minds around this act of terrorism. So terrible an event (we tell ourselves) could not have been the work of humans—it surely must have come at the hands of celestial powers.

The statistics of astrology may seem remote, yet there is a reason why I have referred to it, and I shall explore this later, for there is a relationship between what happens on earth and events in the heavens. For the moment, we might prefer to grasp at the more familiar statistics—the date and time, the type of airplane, the number of passengers and crew, the quantity of fuel it carried. There is a kind of sanity in these statistics that disappears in the horror of statistics that followed. The enormous fireball, thrown through, and out of the building, was caused by the explosion of the volatile fuel. The force of the impact, which was localized between the 87th and 93rd floors, was sufficient to weaken the entire structure of the tower. The heat from the burning aviation fuel was so great that it melted the steel frame of the building. In the interval, another hijacked airplane, United Airlines flight 175, was crashed into the south tower. This act of terrorism occurred at 9:03 A.M., and the structure collapsed in just under an hour. Within less than two hours from the first impact, the entire north tower also collapsed.[2]

More people were to die, in those two hours of violence, than perished in the Revolutionary War, which had lasted for three years.

In 1555, the prophet Michel Nostradamus had written about the Declaration of Independence, which helped give form to an entire civilization (see page 59). How was it possible that he had not foreseen the more direful events in Manhattan, which threaten the freedoms promised in that Declaration?

I write these words from a small village on the edge of the Yorkshire Dales, in England. It is hard to believe that the man-made catastrophe, visited on Manhattan by terrorists during that morning, should have reached its dark shadow as far as this remote English village.

A couple of miles from where I live is a splendid stately home, owned by an acquaintance of mine. Her financier son worked in the commercial section of the World Trade Center, and it is likely that he was in one of the buildings destroyed by the terrorists. Three days have passed since this attack on Manhattan, and still she has had no news of her son. She is one among many suffering thousands, yet, the fact that she is an acquaintance adds a personal poignancy to an event which, I now know, Nostradamus *had* predicted over four hundred years ago.

The act of terrorism has approached my village in another way. Ever since the destruction of the two towers in New York, my fax, e-mail and phone have been busy. I have been contacted by a number of TV and radio broadcasting agencies, all anxious to hear what Nostradamus had predicted about this terrible event.

On Wednesday of the same week I received a fax from a well-known American broadcaster, who works near New York. He sent me a sample verse, for my opinion. According to this correspondent, this verse had been written by Nostradamus during the 16th century. If it had indeed been written at that time, then it was a most remarkable prophecy. The verse seemed to predict the destruction of New York, as it claimed, "in the year of the new century and nine months"—that is, in September 2001.[3]

I had been interviewed on American radio by this broadcaster earlier in the year, when we had discussed the prophecies of Nostradamus, in general. Now, he was anxious to have my opinion about this particular verse: he wanted to know how Nostradamus had been able to predict this terrorism, over four centuries before it occurred.

Even as I received his fax, and recognized the verse as a forgery, I felt sick. It turned my stomach that, within twenty-four hours of so terrible a tragedy, people should be playing with the event in such a way. It seemed to me that, by forging prophecies of this kind, they were actually demoting the catastrophe itself, as though they were anxious to turn it into a kind of superficial game.

I was not the only one to be troubled with this hoax. From a report about the tragedy in *The Sunday Times*, it seems that others had been receiving faxes and e-mails about Nostradamus. The journalist Richard Woods, in an article entitled, "When death came out of the blue," recorded two verses that had been circulating in the United States, allegedly from the pen of the Seer.[4]

Almost immediately after glancing at the fax, I got in touch with the American broadcaster.

"Nothing to do with Nostradamus," I confirmed. "It isn't even a quatrain."

My broadcaster friend did not seem surprised to learn that the verse was a forgery, yet he persisted.

"But, tell me," he ventured, ever alert for a story, "did Nostradamus *ever* predict the destruction of New York in his writings?"

"Not as far as I'm aware," I replied.

At that moment, I was speaking the truth. I had read all the verses of Nostradamus several times, and I could not recall one that predicted the destruction either of Manhattan or New York State.

Even so, my response made me feel strangely inadequate, as though I had left something hanging in the air, something unfinished. I found myself wondering how Nostradamus could possibly have missed such a momentous event. How could he have failed to comment on an event that will certainly change the tenor of civilized life on this planet?

I had read almost everything published on the great Seer, and I knew that the popular books on prophecy constantly misinterpreted his verses. In modern times, it has become a popular pastime to do so, as though Nostradamus were merely intent on predicting the end of the world, or the fiery end of one or another of its major cities. Almost always, the aim of such popular books was to paint a lurid and disturbing image of the future. One presumes that the readership to which these books cater must be more interested in doom and destruction than in a promise of a bright future for mankind.

Such books were far from being works of scholarship. Many individuals who write books about Nostradamus, or circulate his supposed prophecies on the web, know nothing about the methods used by the Savant. Usually, such authors have no substantial knowledge of the 16th-century French, Latin and Greek in which he wrote, and even less understanding of his method of codification. It is unlikely that few of them have even attempted to read the crabbed works of the Master, in the form he penned them.

Among the most inept of these modern authors was Henry C. Roberts, whose book on Nostradamus has sold by the millions, and has ensured that Nostradamus will be misunderstood by whole generations. Now, Roberts *had* interpreted one quatrain as though Nostradamus had foreseen a war between the United States and the Soviet Union, along with the destruction of New York in a nuclear holocaust.[5] Another verse he interpreted as relating to the vicious attack on Pearl Harbor.[6] Yet another he represented as a further prediction of a destructive nuclear catastrophe.[7]

I knew that these were bungled interpretations. They had nothing to do with what Nostradamus had actually written. The first verse did *not* predict a war with the Soviets, nor even the destruction of New York. Indeed, this quatrain I.87 actually dealt with an important phase in the war conducted by the allied American and British armies, in the Mediterranean, during the Second World War.

Quatrain II.54, supposed by Roberts to deal with the Japanese attack on Pearl Harbor, had nothing to do with warfare. It had been written by Nostradamus to describe the first colonial settlement of Jamestown, on the east coast of the New World, in 1607.

The terrible nuclear attack, which Roberts read into quatrain II.91, was an even more foolish interpretation. The French verse really dealt with the future application of electricity, during the 19th century.

Inept as they might have been, such examples of Roberts' commentaries were dangerous. They have persuaded thousands of readers to imagine a series of horrendous events stored up for the Western world, in the not-too-distant future. One end product of the wide circulation of these inept interpretations is that many people really believe that New York will be destroyed in a nuclear explosion. They are convinced that the events at Pearl Harbor had been predicted, and that Nostradamus had foreseen a series of destructive nuclear explosions. It is a moot point whether such fearful expectations actually help engineer the events feared.

I welcome any opportunity to put the minds of such people at rest. Nostradamus did not have in mind such doom-laden prophecies when he wrote these three verses. He had intended each of these verses to which I have referred merely to reveal American efforts and ingenuity in the future. In view of this, I shall give a full translation and commentary for all three quatrains, separately. (See section on Prophecies for America, p. 53.)

In contrast to this impulse to interpret the verses as nothing more than harbingers of doom, Nostradamus himself was fairly optimistic. Very often, he surprised us with rosy descriptions of future events, and it is evident from his writings that he was as much interested in cultural advances as in military conflicts. In fact, one quatrain predicted for the United States a long and successful future, stretching over centuries still to come. It seems to me that the time has arrived when I should examine this optimistic verse, and reveal its meaning.

Besides being a brilliant prophet, Nostradamus was also among the most competent astrologers of the 16th

century. This is why it is commonplace for the wood-
cuts in his books to depict him as a learned philoso-
pher, sitting within a band of the zodiac, or with
planets circling above his head.

This fact, that Nostradamus was a learned astrologer, should be a warning to those who attempt to
understand his verse. The astrology that Nostradamus
used was very different from that with which we are familiar today. This implies that, if we are to understand
his verses, we must familiarize ourselves not only with
astrology, but with a specialized astrology used by savants of the 16th century. This is not the only reason
why it is possible to misunderstand Nostradamus, yet it
is one of the most obvious ones. I have studied Nos-

tradamus for many years, but one thing I know about him is that it is very easy indeed to misinterpret his verses, through ignorance of the century in which he lived, and of the culture to which he belonged.

Spurred on by my conversation with the broadcaster, and by the many faxes and phone calls I had received since the event in New York, I have examined once again the prophetic writings of Nostradamus. Was it possible, I asked myself, that I had missed a quatrain dealing with an attack on Manhattan? Although I have read all the prophecies in his *Prophéties* many times, I know that it is always possible to misunderstand his verses. As a matter of fact, Nostradamus had ensured that no one would be able to understand a single one of his quatrains before that prophecy had unfolded. Was this outrageous act of terrorism included somewhere in the quatrains, awaiting interpretation after the unfolding of the event?

With this question in mind, I sat down and began to re-read all the thousand or so prophetic verses that Nostradamus had published. Between 1555 and 1558, he had written a considerable number of quatrains, or four-lined verses. These, he had claimed, dealt with the future history of the world. His claim was perhaps a little grandiose, as they seemed to deal mainly with the future of Europe, concentrating on events in France and England. However, among the thousand or so verses he did write, about fifty seem to have dealt with the future of what was then called "the New World," of which the United States eventually became the dominant part.

The verses had been arranged by him into groups of a

hundred—which explains why the collection is sometimes referred to as *Centuries*. By 1558, he had completed ten of these books, totaling almost a thousand quatrains in all. However, later editions published as many as twelve books, along with a large number of other verses, abstracted from his published yearbooks, or almanacs.[8]

It is a daunting exercise to attempt a reading of over a thousand obscure verses in the space of one night, yet my efforts were rewarded. Toward the end of the sixth book, I found a quatrain that had always puzzled me. Now, with the advantage of hindsight as a guide, I realized that this verse was one in which Nostradamus had predicted the events of September 2001, in New York.

Later, I rediscovered a second quatrain that had always intrigued me. Hindsight made it apparent that this quatrain was intended to deal with the aftermath of this terrible act of terrorism.

Who was this strange prophet, whose fame has swept down five centuries into the modern world? In many respects, his life has become a mystery to historians, for the few facts that have survived in ancient documents have been overlaid by speculations and imaginative inventions that bear no relationship to historical truth. In the town hall, at Salon, where he spent many years of his life, hangs a portrait of Nostradamus, painted by his eldest son. Whether or not it was a likeness is now hard to tell, but it has been believed, for a very long time, that a woodcut attributed to Leonard Gaultier (see facing page) has caught the appearance of the Prophet more precisely than the painting.[9]

Nostradamus was born at St. Remy, in the south of France, in 1503, and died at Salon, in 1566.[10] He was

born into a family that, two generations earlier, had been forced to convert from Judaism to Christianity. He trained at the medical faculty of Montpellier University, in the south of France, and qualified as a doctor. After traveling for some time, he married and settled down in Salon, in the south of France. From about 1553, he began to write his prophecies. His home in Salon, where he wrote these extraordinary prophecies, and where he practiced medicine and astrology, is now a museum, dedicated to his life and work—a shrine for those who recognize his genius.

Usually, Nostradamus set down his visions in four-lined verses—visionary gems that picked out future events with uncanny precision. In a brief account he left about his methods, he records that, had he wished, he could have written down every detail of the future. There is every reason to believe that this was no idle boast. No one knows how he arrived at his extraordinary visions. In a letter to his patron, King Henri II of France, he merely acknowledged that his knowledge of the future was a gift from God.

It has not always proved easy to understand the products of this God-given gift. Many of the verses of Nostradamus are today as much a riddle as when he was alive. The verse dealing with Manhattan is no exception. The form of this quatrain is so curious that careful commentary will be necessary for any of it to make sense. Nostradamus had intended his verses to be crabbed and incomprehensible—he himself referred to them as *scabrous*, a word which, even in the 16th century, meant "full of obstacles." The French text, as it appears in the 1557 edition, is reproduced at right and illustrates his point perfectly.

We will begin with the original French and its meaning in terms of a fairly literal English translation, as a prelude to explaining its significance. However, Nostradamus was too clever a writer for us to take each of his words *literally*; he wrote in an age when it was commonplace for authors to use secret codes in order to hide their meaning from the prying eyes of the Inquisition. For Nostradamus, as for other savants who wrote in this twilight realm of prediction and astrology, the Inquisition was an ever-present reality. We must always bear in mind the general background of intellectual fear against which the *Prophéties* were written. With these words and in this current climate of apprehension, let us begin.

CENTVRIE VI.

XCVII

Cinq & quarante degrés ciel bruſlera,
Feu approucher de la grand cité neufue,
Inſtant grand flamme eſparſe ſaultera,
Quãt on voudra des normãs faire preuue.

The Attack on Manhattan

•

As we have seen from the French text reproduced earlier, verse 97, from the sixth century of the *Prophéties*, reads:

Cinq & quarante degrés ciel bruslera,
Feu approucher de la grand' cité neufue,
Instant grand flamme esparse saultera,
Quāt on voudra des normās faire preuve.[11]

At a stretch, this could be translated as:

Five and forty degrees the sky will burn,
Fire to approach the great new city,
Within an instant, a great flame will leap like
    lightning,
When one would wish the Normans to give trial.

As we proceed to examine these four lines, we shall discover that neither the French nor the English translation prove to be quite what they seem.

Line One

Cinq & quarante degrés ciel bruslera,

Five and forty degrees the sky will burn,

Nostradamus seems anxious to let us know where the event predicted will take place. He opens his verse with a coordinate that seems indisputable in its precision. It seems that the events to unfold in the prophecy will somehow be linked with a place that falls on 45 degrees latitude.

In modern terms, defining a place by latitude may appear to be ridiculous. However, in the 16th century, it was not at all unusual. For example, in 1585, the explorer Hakluyt wrote a report for Elizabeth I, Queen of England, touching upon the proposed colonization of North America. The title of the document reads:

Inducments to the liking of the voyage intended toward Virginia in 40 and 42 degree of latitude.[12]

An earlier map, probably made in 1580, and which once belonged to Queen Elizabeth's astrological adviser, Dr. John Dee, is of similar interest. This shows Chesapeake Bay and Bermuda, with Raleigh's armorial achievement on part of Virginia. The essential latitude is marked, yet it is not accurate by modern standards.[13]

Nostradamus seems to have been very precise in setting out this coordinate. However, as lines of latitude encircle the globe, they do not afford exact geographic locations. In fact, the latitude of 45 degrees north leaves open several options, none of which seem to include New York. The opening phrase of his verse could be taken as referring to Bordeaux, Turin, and perhaps Cremona and Mantua. In a table of latitudes, published by the astrologer Luca Gauricus, in 1533, a latitude of 45 degrees was ascribed to Venice and Bologna.[14]

Montreal, Canada, is on 45 degrees of latitude by modern standards of measurement.[15] In the ordinary way of things—that is, without clairvoyant vision—Nostradamus could not have known about this city.

The site where Montreal was built had been discovered by Jacques Cartier, in 1535, during the lifetime of Nostradamus. However, it was not until 1611 that it was settled by the French, under the name of Place Royale. It did not become an important city until the 18th century. Even so, if we are to read quite literally the opening lines of the verse as relating to 45 degrees of latitude, then we might be persuaded that Nostradamus had Montreal in mind, rather than New York City.

We now have very accurate maps available of North America and Canada. In modern times, we have little doubt as to the latitude on which Montreal or New York is located. However, as we have seen, things were different in the 16th century. We should be prepared to ask how accurate were the maps of the New World available to Nostradamus.

The eastern seaboard of America had scarcely been explored during the lifetime of Nostradamus. However, the French Huguenots had made attempts to settle in Florida in the 1560s—the decade in which Nostradamus died. That Nostradamus knew in advance about these settlements, and their tragic history, is evident from an extraordinary prophetic quatrain he wrote, in 1562. This prophetic verse dealt with a dramatic, not to say gruesome incident, during the early attempts made by the French to settle Florida and is covered at length in the essay beginning on p. 106.

*   *   *

If we consider this latitude of 45 degrees in terms of maps available to Nostradamus, then we discover something interesting. In a chart of latitude (see below), drawn up in the 16th century, Grenoble (marked G on the chart) is located exactly on 45 degrees.

Marseilles (indicated by M on the chart) is located on 43 degrees. Both these placings are fairly accurate, by modern standards.[16] They were almost certainly based on the coordinates derived from the astrologer-geographer Ptolemy, who lived in the first century of our era. A map of the known Old World, based on these ancient coordinates, is reproduced on page 19.[17] The farther from the ancient center of civilization this map extends, the more inaccurate it becomes. Maps of the 16th century

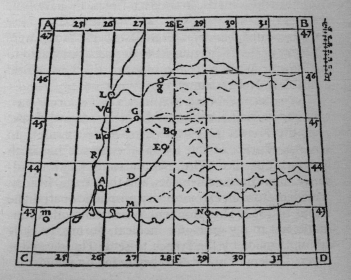

for the newly discovered world were rarely accurate. However, the latitudes for countries around the Mediterranean were fairly accurate. The earliest known map of Florida was one drawn up by an artist-sailor involved in the prophecy made by Nostradamus in 1562. It seems to have been prepared in 1564, and was carefully marked with intervals of latitude. By modern standards, these are between one and three degrees in error.[18] The differences involve only a matter of two degrees or so, yet these discrepancies are sufficient for us to look again at what Nostradamus might have intended by his specific reference to 45 degrees as it pertains to North America.

If we examine a good modern map, we see that 40 degrees of latitude runs between Philadelphia and Baltimore. Washington, D.C., to the south of these, is on 39 degrees.[19]

The city of Boston, the most northerly city from which the terrorists began their terrible mission, lies on 42 degrees.[20]

A map, published by George Best in 1578 (see page 20), shows the St. Lawrence River as a schematic slit, to the north of America. The word *Canada* is marked below this highly schematized river. What is of immediate interest for us is that this map offers some correspondence between the latitudes of Europe (then known without the exactitude we now expect) and America. By modern standards, the map of America that Best drew up is ridiculous. However, the fact is that the corresponding 45 degrees of European latitude (which cuts through Bordeaux, on the western seaboard of the Bay of Biscay, on a map almost certainly known to Nostradamus) corresponds to the area between Florida and the Gulf of St. Lawrence. This offers us a very graphic view of what Nostradamus might have had in

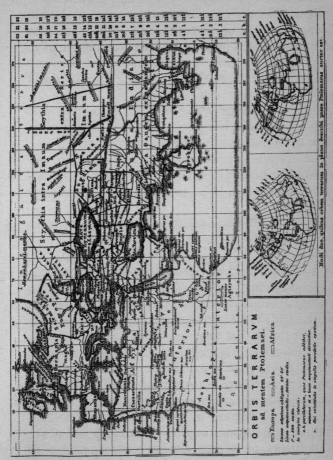

Orbis Terrarum ad mentem Ptolemaei, based on coordinates available in the 15th century, but formulated in the second century.

mind, when he wrote of the specific-sounding 45 degrees.

These maps present, in graphic form, material available to Nostradamus, in the last years of his life. The latter map points to the problem raised by coordinates of latitude, as they were projected in the 16th century, in a very clear way. With this sort of evidence in mind, we might have little difficulty in arguing, without further reading, that Nostradamus had intended to point roughly to that area of land where New York was eventually built. However, we should look more carefully at what he wrote. If we do, then we arrive at a startling conclusion.

The exact-seeming reference in the quatrain is to latitude 45 degrees, which we presume is 45 degrees north. In reference to a prediction about an attack on New York, this is a disappointing coordinate, for, in modern terms at least, it does not mark the latitude of New York City. Forty-five degrees of latitude passes through Nova Scotia, Maine, and Ottawa. New York is on 40 degrees.[21]

If Nostradamus had wanted to specify the location of New York City (which, we presume, he could mysteriously perceive in future centuries), he would surely have given the location as 40 degrees.

It might seem extraordinary to those unfamiliar with the genius of Nostradamus that he was capable of describing things that did not exist in his day, yet this is undeniable. An example of how precisely he worked may be seen from the quatrain in which he revealed the precise day on which World War II would begin.[22] Sometimes, he would even use the personal names of individuals who would not be born for centuries. As we have seen, Hitler's interest in Nostradamus stemmed from a belief that the Seer had named him.[23] There is no doubt at all that Nostradamus had named Hitler's one-time ally, General Franco, and his enemy, General de Gaulle.[24]

It is evident that Nostradamus possessed a remarkable clairvoyance, for he recorded many of the personal names of important figures who would play a part on the stage of history, in the future. All too often, he would encode these names in clever ways within his verses. A good example of this is the encoded reference to the English politician William Pitt, who was so supportive of the American struggle for independence. In this same encoded quatrain, Nostradamus also hid the place name of St. Louis, in Missouri—a city that did not exist in the 16th century.[25] (See the essay beginning on p. 113.)

A hundred similar examples, of Nostradamus providing us with exact dates and precise names for future events, could be listed. Given such accuracy, we might ask why Nostradamus should not have given a similarly precise coordinate for New York City, as being 40 degrees. The answer proves to be a remarkable one. He *does*. If we look at that first line again, we see that he does mention 40 degrees. If we read precisely what he said, then we may translate it as

Five, and forty degrees.

There are two figures here. One is *five*, the other *forty*. Only forty is specified in degrees. This forty degrees (*quarante degrés*) is the precise location of New York City. What, in this context, is *five*, or perhaps *five degrees*? We shall return to this interesting question shortly.

For the moment, let us accept that this reference to forty degrees indicates the location of New York City. What Nostradamus predicts, in this same line, is that the sky above this city will burn. We see, then, that the first line of the quatrain has already introduced the main theme of the events of Tuesday, September 11. This theme is the terrorist act, which began at 42 degrees latitude, in Boston, and ended with those terrible pyrotechnics above New York at 40 degrees latitude.

Just in case it might be argued, by cynics, that I am twisting the words written by Nostradamus, I should set out a few facts. In his quatrains, Nostradamus frequently referred to locations in terms of degrees of latitude: it was a subject that interested him deeply. By an amazing stroke of good fortune, a book dealing with latitudes, and once owned personally by Nostradamus, has recently been discovered in a French library.[26]

In some cases, Nostradamus set out geographical locations in terms of a much earlier system of mensuration—a system of *climata*, derived from Babylonian astrology. Nostradamus was quite open about this, for, in one quatrain, he referred to this system of geographic mensuration as the *climat Babylonique*.[27] Whenever he used this system, he would use a word denoting *clima*. For example, in the enigmatic quatrain V.98, he refers to the climacteric 48 degrees:

> *A quarante huict degré climaterique,*

Without that keyword, he seems *always* to have in mind the 16th-century system, whose correspondence to modern coordinates we discussed previously. In every case where he used the modern method, he gave the figures in a straightforward numeration, not in the poetic mode, "Five and forty."

Line Two

Feu approucher de la grand cité neufue,

Fire to approach the great new city,

[NOTE The word *approucher* is an early version of *approcher* (to approach, or draw near). The final word, *neufue,* is a typical Nostradamian equivalent of *neufe,* the feminine of the French for "new." It is pronounced *neuf,* and therefore rhymes with *preuve.* In some versions of the quatrain, this feminine case is recognized by the marked abbreviation, *grand'*—in this verse, however, the case of *grand* is technically incorrect.]

In some ways, the first and second lines appear to be repetitive. They seem merely to define more closely the place of the predicted catastrophe. In the second line, we find a reference to the great new city (*la grand cité neuve*), which is, in effect, a confirmation that Nostradamus is writing of the latitude on which New York is located. It is unlikely that he would have referred to a "new city," without intending to refer to a city that included *New* in its name. After all, in terms of the 16th century, all cities in North America might be described as new.

Without our interpretation of the latitude, as set out above, it would have been unreasonable to associate the "new city" (*cité neuve*) with New York. In one of his earliest quatrains, Nostradamus had used similar words, *cité neufue*, in a verse that clearly relates to Naples. This place-name is derived from the Greek, *Neopolis*, which meant "new city." The same phrase appears in quatrain X.49, wherein Naples is identified by a number of geological features.[28] However, when the two lines are read together, then the identity of the city is fairly clear.

Given the actual event to which this verse applies, the choice of the infinitive, *approucher*, is brilliant. The fire (*Feu*) is to approach from the sky (*ciel*) specified in the previous line. Anyone who watched, on television, the last seconds of the two planes, directed so dramatically toward the skyscrapers above Manhattan, can appreciate just how apposite are these words of Nostradamus. One moment we saw the airplane—then, within an instant, there appeared a ball of fire, soon hidden beneath a pall of smoke.

In his quatrains, Nostradamus frequently referred to "fire" (*feu*) in the skies. In some cases, these references did point to such things as aerial bombardments, but in other cases they referred to stars, or comets. For example, in quatrain II.46, we have a fire which is actually a comet:

Au ciel veu feu, courant longue estincelle

In the heavens a fire is seen, dragging a tail of sparks.

In this case, the "tail of sparks" helps us identify the particular fire Nostradamus had in mind, for a comet is most easily distinguished by its hairy tail, or *coma*. The literature relating to comets was enormous in the days of Nostradamus (he wrote one book himself, about the effects of the comet of 1559). Usually, the interpretations, and the images attached to them, were bloodthirsty and dramatic. The image on page 26 is from a work published in the middle of the 16th century by the French surgeon Paré.

The reason why Nostradamus referred to comets so frequently in his quatrains was certainly not because he believed them to be harbingers of evil. In most cases, Nostradamus makes such a reference to a comet in order to enable us to date the event he is predicting.

One particular quatrain, which we shall eventually examine in depth, refers to a great fire (*grand feu*), which is nothing more than electricity put to a practical use (see page 92).

The word *feu* is most conveniently translated as "fire," and with this meaning it makes perfect sense within the context of the verse. However, as pointed out, Nostradamus often uses words with one or two related meanings, which add nuances to his verses. The word *feu*

is no exception, for it is a most interesting French word, with a secondary meaning of "defunct," or "dead." It is an interesting word because, although it seems to have continued the ancient meaning of the Latin *functus*, it does appear to have merged, or perhaps confused, with itself the Latin *fatulus*, meaning, "an accomplished destiny," along with the third person, past tense of the French verb, "to be," *il fut*.[29] If we translate it merely as meaning "fire," as in the preliminary translation of the verse (earlier), we lose much of the force of the word. In its ancient French meaning, it contained also the idea of "death dealing," or "mortal," in the sense of something being subject to destiny, which hints at further meaning of the verb *approucher*. Besides describing the approach of fire, Nostradamus is also describing the approach of death and mortality.

Line Three

Instant grand flamme esparse saultera,

*Within an instant, a great flame will leap like
    lightning,*

[NOTE: The case of *grand* seems to be technically incorrect, for it should agree in gender with the feminine of *flamme*. It is perhaps significant that no known version of the quatrain offers the abbreviated version, *grand'*, to denote the feminine case. Interestingly, this abbreviation is found in some examples of the *grand* in the second line of the quatrain: we might reasonably conclude that the contrast drawn between the two was meant to draw our attention to it. We should bear in mind that Nostradamus often used Latin constructions in his quatrains, and, given such a construction, the word *grand* might be intended to unite directly with the verb. An alternative reading of the line will accommodate this notion. We shall also deal with the curious word *esparse* in the main body of text below. The verb *saultera* is a 16th-century equivalent of the modern French *sautera* (he, she or it will leap).]

By any standards, this is a difficult line. It is not easy to understand its full meaning in French, and it is difficult to translate its several ambiguities into English. Perhaps the best we can do is offer several interpretations, each of which seems to be valid:

The word *esparse* is late medieval French, the equivalent of the modern French *épars*, which has several meanings. First, in this context, it is a meteorological term, meaning lightning—though it is a lightning flash that occurs without thunder. By choosing this word, Nostradamus is probably telling us that the flames are not "natural," but man-made.

There is also another meaning to *épars*, derived from the Latin *sparsus*, meaning dispersed, or "sprayed," "sprinkled" or "scattered." The French word means "dispersed here and there," as, for example, in the phrase, *Des débris épars*—debris thrown everywhere. Both meanings combine to suggest, in this context, the great flame of burning aviation fuel that was shot everywhere after the impact, to explode on the instant into flame.

It is not unusual for Nostradamus to intend a word to be read in two or more senses, and in this particular context we have the image of a silent lightning flash overlaid by the idea of a dispersed material or liquid. This is precisely what millions who watched the filmed events saw, as the airplanes crashed into the towers.

The verb *sauter* (here, *saulter*) means "to leap," though in this context it clearly means "leap out." *Saultera* is the future tense, meaning, "it will leap out." With this word, Nostradamus calls to mind the word *sauterelle* (a French word that still means "grasshopper"), which he used in a quatrain that is believed to refer to helicopters. Here, in this quatrain, the word helps paint a picture of a great sheet of flame leaping through the skies, like soundless lightning.

In terms of grammar, the genders of the words used in this line are inaccurate. Properly speaking, the great flame should be *grande flamme*, as the noun is feminine.

In spite of this deviation, Nostradamus has insisted (quite correctly) on making *esparse* feminine, with a final *e*. Does *esparse saultera* (perhaps meaning "the lightning will leap," or, "it will leap in a scattered fashion") merely extend the image of the great flame (*grand flamme*)? Or is it constructed to hide another meaning?

With these points in mind the line might be construed as meaning:

Within the instant, from the great [building?] will leap . . . flame.

I have proposed that the missing noun is "building" because it helps make sense of the verse as a whole. However, I have to observe that Nostradamus frequently used the word *grand* (or its feminine counterpart, *grande*) as a noun. In this case, he had in mind "grand people," such as aristocrats or important politicians: we shall see examples when we examine his predictions about heavier-than-air flight in the essay beginning on page 131. In this context, however, those words would make no sense at all, given that the events are supposed to be unfolding in the skies. "Building" fits with the sense of this line.

Esparse is a strange word, even for a 16th-century writer. Normally, when Nostradamus was intent on describing fire in the skies, he would use the more conventional word *foudre*, meaning "lightning." For example, in verse VIII.2, which relates to a war in France, he wrote:

Foudre, grand gresle, mur tombe dans Garonne.

Lightning, great hail, [the] wall falls into the Garonne.

We must ask why Nostradamus has been so obscure about a detail of imagery which did not, in itself, demand obscurity. Even the strangeness of its construction would suggest that it is, in fact, designed to hide something. The words *flamme esparse* are unique to the verse we are presently considering. It is important that we bear this in mind, as the two words may enclose a code.

At the time of writing, only the names of the terrorists have been published. There is a great deal of speculation as to which terrorist cell they belonged, as to who their leader is, and as to which country has financed them. These two words might sweep aside all speculation. They may be interpreted in such a way as to identify a locality. The strangely united *esparse saultera* could have been constructed by Nostradamus to disguise the word *parses*.

esPARSE Sautera[30]

Nowadays, the word *Parses* might be taken as a reference to Persia, perhaps to the Parsees.[31] Nostradamus used the word *Perce* in a quatrain, where he was evidently referring to the Persians—those of modern Iran.[32] In another quatrain, he refers to the "head of Persia" (*Le chef de Perse*), clearly indicating that he had in mind not a king, but a leader such as the Imam.[33] On the Ptolemaic map, reproduced on page 19, the country is named Persis. In the medieval world, *Parses* had a different application.

From ancient geographers, we learn that the Parses were those from Pasira (sometimes Parsira, sometimes Bagisara). This locality was in ancient Gedrosia, in Asia. Where this latter country was supposed to be located, in terms of European geography, may be seen from the Ptolemaic map. Gedrosia is centered (quite wrongly, as it happens) on latitude 25 degrees north, and longitude 110 degrees east. Formerly, this large area incorporated the southeastern corner of Persia and the northwestern area of Pakistan. In the opinion of the historian of ancient geography William Smith, Pasira included the borders of Seistan and the kingdom of Kabul, a province in what is now Afghanistan. The kingdom of Kabul (spelled *Cabul*) is on the Ptolemaic map, which is based on second-century AD geography, at the approximate location of 33 north, 115 east.[34]

This interpretation of a hidden structure within the two words *esparse saultera* may seem forced, yet the truth is that Nostradamus *did* use such simple codifications in his quatrains. Furthermore, he frequently referred to countries and regions by their ancient names, used in available geographies. Almost certainly, he would have had the name Pasira, or one of its several variants, from a reading of, or commentary upon, the *Indica* of the second-century Greek geographer Flavius Arrianus.[35]

If this is an encoding—and the strangeness of the line suggests that it is—then we may take it that Nostradamus is pointing to the region of Afghanistan. The coding is perfect, for it is integrated into words implying that the terrible destruction wrought by these men will leap, and spread out. Perhaps the destruction will spread out more widely into the world than they ever imagined.

Line Four

Quāt on voudra des normās faire preuve.

When one would wish the Normans to give trial

[NOTE: *Quāt* is an old-form abbreviation, the modern form of which is *Quand* (When). Similarly, *normās* is an old-form abbreviation, the modern form of which is *Normans*. In some versions of the quatrain, *preuve* is given as *preuue*.]

The keyword *Normans* deflects a superficial analysis of this quatrain. The word today suggests Normandy, in northern France. Within the framework of the quatrain, read prior to the Manhattan event, the verse seemed to be very simple. The fact that 45 degrees cuts through southern France—skirting Bordeaux to the west and Valence to the east—seemed to mark the southern extremity, while Normandy marked the northern. For this reason, whenever I read the quatrain, prior to September 2001, I imagined that it related to some event in France, either between these two extremes, or close to the more southerly latitude.

However, it is typical of Nostradamus to misdirect his readers in such a way. His purpose is always to make his verse impenetrable, before the event prophesied helps make some sense of the quatrain.

In light of the terrible events in New York, what are we to make of this word *Normans*? When we examine it closely, we are astonished at its extraordinary aptness. The first definition of the term is, of course, "people who live in the North." The word, though French in itself, is probably derived from a combination of the English *north*, and *man*. In the 16th century, when Nostradamus wrote the quatrains, these men of the North (sometimes, even in modern French, called Northmans), were pirates. This sense is generally included in all good French dictionaries.[36] However, we need look no further than Nostradamus for a use of the word *Normans* in the context of piracy, for it appears in several of his quatrains, with this meaning. For example, in quatrain VII.10, he writes of *Normans* acting as pirates in the Mediterranean.

> *Normans,*
> *Caspre passer Barcelone pillé isle.*

> *Normans,*
> *In vessels of Corsairs to pass Barcelona, ravage the isle.*[37]

Pirates are, of course, terrorists, intent on using fear and terror to gain their personal objectives.

Now, the first thing that strikes us about this reference to Normans is that those who hijacked the airplanes, with the intention of crashing them into the two towers in New York, were certainly pirates. They had boarded the crafts with the intention of taking them over by force. Like the pirates who once ravaged the seven seas, they were merciless, and quite prepared to kill the captain, crew and passengers of the craft they boarded. Perhaps we should take it as a mere coincidence that some of these terrorists trained at the flying school in Norman, Oklahoma.

They were pirates, but it remains to be seen whether they were, strictly speaking, "Men from the North." In terms of latitude, the city of Kabul is 5 degrees south of latitude 40. However, since the two airplanes that were crashed into the two towers of the World Trade Center began their flights from Boston, then it is evident that these hijackers did sweep down from the north.

What are we to make of the curious words *faire preuve*, which end the quatrain? The implications behind these two words are fascinating. They point to legalistic methods popular in the medieval period, yet dispensed with long ago. In former times, under prescribed circumstances, those accused of certain crimes were permitted to endure a particular form of judgment to prove their innocence or guilt. The idea behind this kind of trial was that God was to make judgment, rather than men—God would ensure that the trial undertaken by the accused would result in a sound judgment. Some of these trials, or *preuves*, were barbarous, and seemed little removed from torture. For example, the accused might, willingly, place his or her hand into a vat of boiling water for a given number of seconds. If the hand emerged unscathed, he or she was pronounced "not guilty"—the person was *proven* innocent. One form of this special trial has come down to modern times in the phrase "trial by combat."

The hijackers themselves are beyond earthly judgment, and we must presume that the *preuve* does not apply to them. For certain, they will have another judgment to face. Are we to assume from the Nostradamus reference to trial that those who were ultimately responsible for this terrible crime will themselves be brought before justice? Or does the phrase refer to the military combat that will surely be the direct outcome of their actions? Nostradamus appears to be of the opinion that such a form of combat, or *preuve*, will take place.

This brings us back to the first line's mention of the number five, which, as was suggested earlier, might have particular significance.

If we were right to separate the five (*Cinq*) from the forty (*quarante*), and to claim that the number five has nothing to do with degrees, it is reasonable to wonder how it is connected.

When I first started writing about this catastrophe, in terms of the Nostradamus quatrain, I did not know about the identities of the terrorists. It was not until September 14 that I became aware of the names of the five terrorists who had crashed the first passenger-laden airplane into the World Trade Center. However, by that time I had already written most of what you have just read.

I had begun to suspect, from the structure of the first line of the quatrain, that there must have been five terrorists on the first flight—perhaps even on the second flight, also.

On the night of the 14th, the FBI published the names of the first five, thus confirming my original impression, based on my reading of the verse.[38] The same report suggested (though there is presently some doubt about it) that there were also five on the plane that destroyed the second tower of the World Trade Center.

In light of this information, we can begin to see how brilliantly Nostradamus encoded what he foresaw. Loosely interpreted, the line could read:

> *Five [terrorists] and [at] forty degrees the sky will burn.*

The Consequences of
September 11, 2001

•

Earlier, we noted that there was a second quatrain that seemed to deal with the consequences of the disaster. Perhaps it is intended to develop the idea of the *preuve* that ends the verse we have just examined?

It is at this juncture that we should note that Nostradamus himself pointed out that he had constructed his verses to make it impossible to understand them before the event predicted had occurred. In this case, however, it does look like there is one verse that almost identifies itself as being a commentary on the consequences of the disaster in Manhattan.

Without any of the security offered by hindsight, let us look at quatrain II.81, which was first published in 1555, and which seems to reflect on the dire consequences of the terrorist act of 2001. The second verse is reproduced here, to show how it appeared, during the lifetime of Nostradamus. The following quatrain was published in 1557:

L X X X I

Par feu du ciel la cité presque aduste,
Vrna menasse encor Ceucalion.
Vexé Sardaigne par la punique fuste,
Apres que Libra lairra son Phaëton.

In modern setting, the French of quatrain II.81 reads:

Par feu du ciel la cité presque aduste,
Urna menasse encor Ceucalion,
Vexé Sardaigne par la punique fuste,
Apres que Libra lairra son Phaëton.[39]

This is one of the few verses which lends itself well to
line-by-line analysis since it is a very unified quatrain:
Nostradamus had made use of Greek mythology to
portray particular events following the burning of a
city. Since the sources of all these mythological references are known, it is as good for me to reveal them,
line by line, before glancing at the quatrain as a whole.

First Line

Par feu du ciel la cité presque aduste,

The city almost burned by fire from the sky

For the moment, we shall assume that this *cité aduste*
(burned city) is a reference to the recently attacked
Manhattan—the *cité neufue* of quatrain VI.97. It is a
daring assumption, for, given the human predilection
for reciprocal destruction, and the power of modern

weaponry, *many* cities might be described as having been destroyed by fire from the sky. At first glance, the verse could apply to London or Coventry, Berlin or Dresden—indeed, to a hundred cities in Europe, caught up in the horrors of World War II. However, as the examination of the quatrain proceeds, this assumption does prove to be reasonably sound.

While this burning city undoubtedly was a vision of the future for Nostradamus, the imagery in the quatrain is derived from the remote past. Ovid's exquisite poem *Metamorphoses* contains the story of how the son of the Sun sets the whole world aflame. This youth is Phaethon, who is arrogant enough to believe that he can drive the horses of the Sun, in their daily course through the heavens. The uncontrolled chariot of the Sun plunged from its accustomed route, set fire to the earth below, destroyed the cities of the earth, and even threatened the stability of the Heavens. Ovid wrote this marvelous series of mythological stories around the beginning of the first century. From the evidence of the extent to which he used these stories in his quatrains, we imagine that Nostradamus must have been particularly fond of Ovid; he certainly appears to have appreciated much of the hidden symbolism in his work.[40] The use of the *Metamorphoses* to reflect upon the destiny of America, is particularly appropriate, as this poem was the first substantial work to be translated on North American soil. The poet and traveler George Sandys had translated part of it during his tedious and storm-troubled voyage to Virginia (where he was to be the first treasurer of the Colony) in 1621.

The story told by Ovid, in the context of this burned

city, is highly relevant to the quatrain: indeed, the French word *aduste* (burned) that appears in the first line seems designed to reflect the Latin *adustus*, which has the same meaning, and which appears several times in the Ovidian text. Furthermore, in the last line of the quatrain, the youth responsible for this burning is mentioned by name. Essentially we should note that, in Ovid's poem, the conflagration of the world is a direct consequence of the youth's arrogance:

> *Whole cities with their ramparts blaze,*
> *And peopled kingdoms turn to ashy haze;*
> *Mountains with their living forests burn . . .*[41]
>   (Ovid, *Metamorphoses*, pp. 215 ff. Translation by author.)

That Nostradamus should adopt such a theme, as a consequence of the terrorist act recorded in the quatrain we have just analyzed, is itself a cause for concern. We must conclude that Nostradamus considers the consequences of the Manhattan terrorism as having a dire effect on the world as a whole.

As we shall discover, the entire quatrain is itself written around themes of ancient times. The second and fourth lines deal with yet other myths recounted from Ovid's *Metamorphoses*. The fourth line is a reference to ancient history, which merges into myth.

Why should Nostradamus weave a four-line verse around ancient themes, when he is pointing to an event that would occur in 2001 AD? The simple reason for this is that, in each case, the myth recounted is one that begins with a tragedy, moves through catastrophe, yet concludes in a redemptive success. One cannot help concluding that this is what Nostradamus sees as the consequence to the attack on Manhattan, on September 11, 2001—renewal and triumph.

The first line appears to offer few problems—it is a straightforward description of an unnamed city almost burned to cinders (*presque aduste*). It is with the second line that our problems begin.

Second Line

Urna menasse encor Ceucalion,

Urna menaces once more Ceucalion,

The second line drops us, fairly and squarely, into the realms of ancient Greek mythology. Before examining its hidden meaning, we must look to the greatest challenge of all in linguistic terms: what is, or who is, Ceucalion? There is no such figure in mythology, or in recorded history, yet it is definitely the word that appeared in the first few editions of the *Prophéties*. By 1668, editors who under most circumstances remained faithful to the Nostradamian texts appear to have lost patience with the meaningless word. About that time, some editor, or printer, changed it to Deucalion—the name of a famous mythological figure, sometimes wrongly described as the Greek Noah.[42] I happen to agree with this change. It seems apparent that Ceucalion was a misspelling, and Nostradamus had in mind the story of Deucalion, which we shall examine shortly.

Who is the Urna that "yet again menaces Deucalion"? *Urna*, as the astrologer Nostradamus knew full well, is one of the Latin names for the zodiacal sign Aquarius.[43] The name is derived from the fact that this sky god always carries an urn, within which are supposed to be the sacred Waters of Life. Sometimes, as in the figure reproduced below, the waters pour into an overflowing bowl.

In this second line, Nostradamus seems to visualize Aquarius pouring his ample waters on the earth, in such a way as to *menace* Deucalion. This *menacing* of Deucalion points to the story of the ancient Flood, a story that came into Greek mythology from Egypt, in which Mankind is threatened with extermination. Once again, this is a myth recounted by Ovid in his *Metamorphoses*.[44]

In the ancient forms of astrology, Aquarius was more intimately linked with the idea of floods than in

modern times. The historian of star lore R.H. Allen records that Aquarius was associated with the month *Shabatu*, "the Curse of Rain." In the Babylonian *Epic of Creation*, in that part of the book corresponding to this constellation, is an account of the World Deluge, proving that, in ancient times, Aquarius was linked with the notion of the World Deluge. In Babylonian astrology, Aquarius was known as *Gu*, an overflowing water jar. No doubt the *Urna* of Greek and Roman astrology was derived from this source.[45]

In the myth recounted by Ovid, it was not Aquarius who poured these waters, but Zeus. The story tells how Zeus was outraged by Lycaeon, the king of Arcadia. The latter had slain a hostage, and offered his roasted flesh to Zeus, merely to establish whether or not he really was a god. In punishment Zeus turned Lycaeon into a wolf-man. His anger at the human race unabated, Zeus decided to flood the world and destroy mankind.

Deucalion, the son of Prometheus, was advised by his father to build an ark to survive the Flood. Having done this, he and his wife, Pyrrha, floated in their life raft above the waves, until the waters had subsided. Perhaps Nostradamus has this survival in mind when introducing the idea of Aquarius (*Urna*), for this is the Age which is to come. In the sequence of cosmic ages, that of Aquarius follows the Age of Pisces, in which we presently live.

That the new age will be different from the old is perhaps hinted at in the continuation of the Greek myth.[46] When the land was dry, Deucalion received a message from the oracle of Themis. The surviving pair was instructed by the oracle to cast behind them the bones of their mother. The essence of the story is that only after some time did Deucalion realize that "the bones of his mother" were a reference to the stone of the earth.[47] The pair did as instructed. The stones thrown by Deucalion changed into men. Those thrown by Pyrrha turned into women. Thus, Nostradamus seems to imply that, with the Age of Aquarius, the race of Mankind will be transformed.

Although Nostradamus does not spell out this detail of the myth in his quatrain, it is implicit in his mention of the ancient Flood, and the urn of Aquarius.

The transition from the destructive sky fires (of the first line) to the destructive waters of the second line is a fairly subtle one, and may puzzle the modern reader. However, an informed reader of the 16th century would not be puzzled by this transition. The fact is that Deucalion had been the son of Prometheus, who had stolen fire from the gods, to make it available to mankind. The fire that had been intended to benefit humanity had been changed into one that almost destroyed the world. Just so, for example, was the liquid aviation fuel—so essential to civilized life— transformed into a fireball over the city of New York, rendering the area *aduste*.

Third Line

Vexé Sardaigne par la punique fuste,

Sardinia vexed by the Carthaginian sail,

Sardaigne is the French for Sardinia, the island in the Mediterranean. The word *punique* is French for

Carthaginian—the inhabitants of Carthage, on the north coast of Africa. The word *fuste* is late medieval French for "sail," or "ship."

The line seems to point back to the very beginning of history in Sardinia, when the invading Carthaginians sailed across the Mediterranean, and took over the island. The Sardinians may well have been vexed to find their lands wrested from them by the Carthaginians, but the truth is that these interlopers brought with them a far superior civilization, which lasted for some centuries. It is in this account—of a new beginning for mankind, a new age—that we find a link between this enigmatic third line and the previous two. It is utterly fascinating that the period during which the Carthaginians held Sardinia corresponds to the two and a half centuries that Nostradamus sees, in another quatrain, as lying, like a promised land, for the civilization of North America.

In terms of this other quatrain (see page 38), the period from the "fire" (2001) to the end of the Solar Age, in 2236 AD, is 235 years. The precise length of the Carthaginian culture in Sardinia is not known, but it has been estimated at about two and a half centuries.[48]

Fourth Line

Apres que Libra lairra son Phaëton.

After which Libra will drop her Phaethon.

In the final line of the verse we are introduced to yet another mythological figure. Like Urna, Libra is a zodiacal sign and a constellation, drawn by the stars. The figure is usually portrayed as a female holding a pair of scales—sometimes as a pair of scales alone.

Libra may at first seem out of place in this verse. While she fits into the general cosmic imagery derived from Ovid's poem, she is mentioned neither in the story of Deucalion, nor, it seems, does she appear in the story of Phaethon. However, this is not quite the truth. In the midst of Phaethon's unruly journey through the heavens, he sees the monstrous shapes of beasts through which he must travel. These are the constellations. Ovid picks out one in particular, which is the fearsome asterism, Scorpius, with its claws and tail:

> *There is a Place above, where Scorpio bent*
> *In Tail and Arms surrounds a vast Extent;*
> *In a wide Circuit of the Heav'ns he shines,*
> *And fills the Space of Two Coelestial Signs*
> (Translation by Addison, from the 1720 edition of the
> *Metamorphoses*, II. 198ff.)

Ovid does not mention Libra by name, *yet she is present in this description.* Hidden in these three lines is a reference to Libra that Ovid's readers, and a 16th-century scholar such as Nostradamus, would immediately recognize. In the old star maps, the Scorpion's claws were, in ancient times, often called *chelae*, and were distinguished from the Scorpion itself.[49] *Chelae*, or the "claws," was later called Libra. This constellation of Scorpius, where "two signs of heaven crossed," was depicted well into late medieval imagery as a scorpion grasping in its claws the balance of Libra. The following woodcut appeared in a work published during the lifetime of Nostradamus.

This traditional imagery implies that the Libra, to

which Nostradamus refers, is that in the *claws* of Scorpius, as mentioned by Ovid. What do these Libran claws of Scorpius do to Phaethon?

In Ovid's poem, Phaethon is in the heavens, vainly attempting to control the chariot of the Sun with the four reins, when he encounters some of the sky monsters—the more threatening of the constellational creatures. At the sight of the twin-signed Scorpius, Phaethon is so terrified that he finally loses all control:

> *Half dead with sudden Fear he dropt the Reins;*
> *The Horses felt 'em loose upon their Mains,*
> *And, flying out through all the Plains above,*
> *Ran uncontroul'd were-e'er their Fury drove;*
> *Rush'd on the Stars, and through a pathless Way*
> *Of unknown Regions hurry'd on the Day.*
> *And now above, and now below they flew,*
> *And, near the Earth the burning Chariot drew.*

> (Translation by Addison, from the 1720 edition of the
> *Metamorphoses, II. 198ff.*)

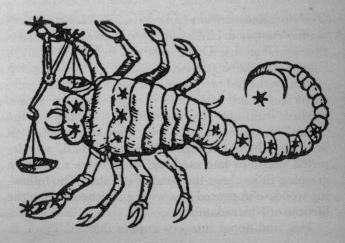

Nostradamus seems to be pointing to a period, after the terrorist act in Manhattan, during which everything will be out of control. Just as Phaethon, cramped by fear, loses control, so will those responsible for civilized life.

After the coming of the Carthaginian sails (that is, of a new form of civilization), Libra, the ruler of harmony and peace, will *lairra* Phaethon. The mad celestial career of this audacious youth, as he sets the world to destructive flames, will come to an end. It is perhaps after this period that the two and a half centuries of peace, suggested in the third line, will materialize.

The full meaning of the last line seems to hang upon precisely what the verb *lairra* means. The translation used here means "will drop," but this suggestion has involved a good deal of guesswork. It could mean, more precisely, "will abandon."[50] Libra will abandon her Phaethon, and he will fall to his death. This is the outcome of events described by Ovid. Having lost control of the horses of the Sun, Phaethon is dragged, helpless, through the burning world, causing mayhem wherever he goes. At length, to bring an end to the conflagration and carnage, Zeus shoots the boy, with one of his thunderbolts. The boy falls from the skies, dead. After this cosmic catastrophe, even the Sun god is reluctant to return to his duties, yet eventually he does so. The cycle of time is renewed, and the Earth is healed.

From our standpoint, one detail of this symbolism is of deep interest. The further destruction of the world is stopped by the god Zeus, with his thunderbolt. Nostradamus may well have recognized the deeper relevance of this god to the events in America. As we may see from the picture on the next page, the attribute of Zeus (seated to the extreme left) is an eagle. This may not be an American eagle, yet it may be taken as a supportive symbolism of the meaning behind Ovid's story. Did Nostradamus recognize the role of the American eagle, in bringing to an end this wild career of an arrogant youth, who infected the whole world with his unreasonable ambitions?

It is not too imaginative to see this fascinating reworking of mythology as relating to the United States. The fire from heaven promises a new beginning, a new Aquarian age. The citizens of this modern age may look with some disdain or alarm on the idea that their life-style is to change. Somehow, the consequences of the terrorist act will lead to a Phaethon-like excess which will, figuratively, one hopes, set the world on fire. However, in the finale, this will lead to an ultimately beneficial change in civilized life.

What are we to make of the background to this quatrain? We are, of course, tempted to read it as a blood and thunder prophecy. Nostradamus is mingling the stories of Deucalion and Phaethon, both of which clearly relate to disasters. Furthermore, there is a hint at a new or coming age in the former story. This notion of a new age is emphasized in particular in the tale of Deucalion, because Ovid preceded this story with an account of the Ages of Mankind. Are we to take this flooding and burning of the world as a prediction of a great war, or as a forecast of a new age?

Ovid's work deals with change and transformation, and many of his metamorphoses are strange and unexpected. For this reason alone, it is reasonable to anticipate that the events predicted within the quatrain will be strange and unexpected in their outcome. As pointed

out already, the stories of Deucalion and Phaethon begin as catastrophes, yet conclude on a redemptive note.
One cannot help feeling that, behind the imagery of
the quatrain, with its hints at a world ablaze, the prediction within the quatrain is intended to point to
something redemptive. It is true that the arrogant
youth who caused all this trouble is shot down; the solar chariot returns to its earlier diurnal rhythm, and the
earth heals. It is also true that the father—the Sun
god—loses a son. Yet we must not forget that it was the
father's own irresponsibility and foolishness that allowed Phaethon to drive the dangerous chariot of the
Sun. There are many themes here—the loss of kin, the
interlude of the burning earth, the just killing of the
son, the irresponsibility of the father, lack of proper
control, even the search for identity. There are many

themes, and it is not at all easy to determine which of these Nostradamus is seeking to develop in terms of a prediction.

From where we stand, prior to the unfolding of the event, there are several possible interpretations, yet none of them may be accurate. For example, if we were to regard Libra (a figure of Justice with the Scales) as a reference to the United States, then this lends itself in a compelling way to a most interesting interpretation. In terms of the final line of the quatrain, the Phaethon that Libra lets fall could be symbolic of terrorists, or of those ultimately responsible for the acts of terrorism. In this case, it was the terrorists who burned up the earth, and were shot down by the just thunderbolt. This kind of speculation is not entirely fruitless, yet it is unlikely to lead us into an accurate assessment of how the future will unfold.

Nostradamus always surprises our expectations in his quatrains. For this reason alone, it would be rash, at this point, to read into the verse too deeply merely in terms of blood and thunder. It does appear that we will see the meaning of this quatrain begin to unfold over the next few months.

Prophecies
for America

Declaration of Independence

•

One of the more remarkable verses from the 1558 edition of the *Prophéties* is IX:47, which deals with one of the most historically significant documents in American history—the Declaration of Independence. The French runs:

> *Les soussignez d'indigne delivrance,*
> *Et de la mulcte auront contrire advis,*
> *Changé monarque mis en pareille trense,*
> *Serrez en cage se verront vis à vis.*[51]

As is often the case with Nostradamus, translation is not easy. There is no French, Latin, Provençal or Greek word *trense* (see third line). Therefore, one can assume that it is either a Nostradamian version of *transe*, a rare singular of *transes*, "fear," or that it is from the Greek, with a meaning that will be explored later. The tentative translation, below, employs the Greek version.

> *The signers of delivery from an unworthy situa-*
> *tion,*

> *The legal consequences will have contrary opin-*
> *ions,*
> *Change monarch put in equal clarity,*
> *Those kept in a cage they will see themselves face to*
> *face.*

"The undersigned" (*Les soussignez*) is likely a reference to those who signed the Declaration. It was a document designed to effect the deliverance of America from an unworthy condition (*d'indigne delivrance*). The French *indigne* means "unworthy," or "a shameful condition." We shall see, shortly, that, in keeping with the idea of a formal document, there is a legalistic element in the quatrain, and this alerts us to the fact that there is a specifically legal sense to the word. *Indigne* can mean "disqualified," in the sense that one might be disqualified from an inheritance (*indigne de succéder*).

One codification in this verse is very remarkable. In the popular mind, the Declaration of Independence was *signed* on July 4, 1776. However, as all historians report, this was not the case. There may be no doubt that celebrations in recognition of independence were held on that auspicious date, but the Declaration itself was not signed on that day, even though the document does bear that date.[52]

Even the official account of the Declaration recognizes this truth, as the following quotation confirms:

> *The record shows that Congress entered upon direct consideration of the question of independence July 1, 1776, by voting to resolve itself into a committee of the whole to take into consideration the resolution introduced by Richard Henry Lee, and to refer*

the draft of the declaration to this committee. Benjamin Harrison, a member from Virginia, was called to the chair, and after a prolonged debate consuming the entire day the resolution was adopted. The committee of the whole then rose, and the president, Mr. Hancock, resumed the chair, whereupon Mr. Harrison reported that the committee had adopted the resolution. The House voted to postpone action on the resolution as reported until the next day, July 2, on which date the resolution was adopted. So that the real independence day is the 2d of July. Upon the adoption of the resolution Congress resolved itself immediately into the committee of the whole, "to consider draft of a Delaration of Independence, or the form of announcing the fact to the world." Debate on the draft continued through the 3d and 4th of July.[53]

The final draft was prepared on the evening of the 4th. On the following day, printed copies, authenticated by the signatures of John Hancock and Charles Thompson, were sent to the governors of the states, and to the commanding officers of the American armies. It was to be read to the public, from the Philadelphia State House yard, on July 8. On July 9, George Washington had the Declaration read before each brigade of his army. However, it was not until August 2 that signing began, though the last six signatures were not finally in place until 1781.[54]

In spite of this history of the document itself, July 4, 1776, is etched into the national consciousness, and it is this date which is found at the head of the Declaration itself. The disparity between the two dates is significant because Nostradamus seems to have been aware of the second date, over two hundred years earlier. This is suggested from the numerology he adopted for the quatrain. He has placed the verse as 47 in the sequence. Given Nostradamus' numerology, this may be interpreted as the 4th day of the 7th month. In the Gregorian calendar, which we now use, and which was used at the time of the Declaration (but which was not used in the time of Nostradamus), this is July 4.[55] Now, this 47th verse is in book 9. If we add together 47 and 9, we obtain 56. This is the total number of signers of the Declaration, as may be seen from the collection of signatures on the Declaration itself (see facing page).

Mulcte (in the second line) is an interesting word, in this context of the Declaration, for it has a legal undertone. In general, the verb refers to mulcting, or to ordering a legal fine, but, in this case, Nostradamus uses it as a noun. The words *la mulcte* must mean something like "the fine," or "the legal consequence," and it is in this latter sense that we will interpret it. Nostradamus tells us that the legal consequences will have, or will attract, contrary opinion (the old French *advis* is the equivalent of the modern French *avis*, "opinion," or "judgment"). The line seems to suggest that there will be many (perhaps, legal) opinions as to the consequence of the promulgation of the Declaration, among the *soussignez*.

In fact, this proves to have been the case. It may seem odd, in retrospect, yet the truth is that the majority of Americans did not want a complete break with Britain. This is evident in the great number of loyalists who fought with the British army. It is even true to say that not all the "signers" were happy with the consequences of their actions. Whatever their personal opinion (*advis*), they signed because they represented states

In CONGRESS. July 4, 1776.

that had voted for secession from Britain.[56] Even after the Declaration, Robert Morris, one of the signers for Pennsylvania, seemed to be questioning the idea of independence, which, he felt, would not "redound to the honor of America."[57] It is no accident that one fascinating modern study of the attitude of Congress, at this point in history, is called, *The Reluctant Rebels*.[58]

Henry Laurens, the vice president of the state of South Carolina, was not alone in seeing the break with Britain as an "awful renunciation of a union." Aware of the great difficulties in finding support for the Revolution in his state, Laurens concluded that, "in my private opinion, Congress had been too hasty in shutting the door against reconciliation [with Britain]."[59] Once the conflict had begun (and much to the despair of George

Washington), many individuals seemed prepared to seek an accommodation with the British, and the number of loyalists increased. It is sometimes said that, in New York, the loyalists were more numerous than the rebels. Joseph Reed, the American adjutant general, confessed to a friend that he could not see the point of risking what he saw as "the fate of America" in attempting to defend the city of New York, the greater part of whose inhabitants were for the British.[60]

What are we to make of the last half of the quatrain? The issue behind the signing of the Declaration was, of course, involved with the changing of the monarchy (*change monarque*), as Nostradamus indicated, with such wonderful conciseness, in the second line. The Monarchy, in the figure of George III, was a symbol of the distant control and arbitrary lawmaking with which the Americans wished to dispense. In four words, Nostradamus sets out what these rebels sought to replace the monarchy with:

mis en pareille trense

The word *pareille* touches the nub of the issue behind the rebellion. As the Declaration itself put it, the Americans sought "equality." The famous phrase, from the text of the Declaration, is "all men are created equal." The French *pareille* means "likeness," but the fact that Nostradamus has represented it in the feminine case (*pareil* is the masculine version) invites us to equate it with *la égalité* (equality), which was to be the street cry of the French revolutionaries.

What are we to make of the word *trense*, which is not found in any dictionary? It seems that Nostradamus is coining a new word from a Greek term, τρανης (*tranes*), meaning "clear," "distinct," and even "bright."

With the Declaration itself in mind, we might even be tempted to read the word as meaning "self-evident," in the sense that it was utterly clear.

The consequence of the signing is set out in the fourth line of the verse. *Serrez* must be read as *serrés* (a reminder that Nostradamus frequently left out accents, in order to add an element of ambiguity to his words). The phrase *vis à vis* must be read in its Latin sense of *visum, visus* ("sight, face," or "face to face"), to give the meaning:

> *Those kept in a cage will see themselves face to*
> *face.*

It would be easy to misread this line, and to see it as referring to the campaign of delays established by both the reluctant Lord Howe, and by the clever George Washington. However, my further consideration leads us to believe that the line refers to the cages, or straight-jackets, in which both Howe and Washington were placed by circumstances.

Lord Howe was trapped by the restrictions placed upon him by the British government. In the first years of the war, he had the opportunity to wipe out the American army, held together, seemingly, by little other than the willpower of George Washington. Time and again, Howe allowed the Americans to escape, perhaps feeling that an utter rout would create a resentment that would prevent the British from ever again ruling in America. In effect, Howe's trap lay in the ambiguity of his role. He was a peacemaker (which followed his own inclination), yet at the same time, he was represented in the contradictory role as General, with almost 30,000 troops under his command, already on American soil. His attempts to lay peace proposals before George Washington, the commander of the American forces, were stymied by the fact that, legally, he was not permitted to negotiate with the rebels. He could not address Washington as "General," and the Americans refused to recognize whom he meant when he addressed letters to Mr. Washington.[61] These formalities were tight straitjackets, which bound Howe into a role he did not really wish to play.

For their part, the Americans were trapped (*Serrez en cage*) by the fact of the Declaration itself. In their eyes, the document had unilaterally severed contact with British politics and regal control. In their eyes, King George III, and his representatives, no longer had jurisdiction in America. When, as late as August 1776, Howe wrote to Benjamin Franklin offering yet another olive branch, Franklin rightly pointed out that any suggestion whereby America undertook to submit to Britain was futile. Both men were imprisoned in their legal positions, and Franklin must have known that the consequences of his words could be nothing other than war. At the time of this correspondence, Howe had over 30 men-of-war and about 400 transports moored on waters outside New York. It was the largest fleet ever seen in America, and, up to that time, the largest army ever sent from British shores.[62]

Perhaps the most wonderful thing about this last line of the quatrain is the choice of the word "cage." With its association with imprisonment, it is absolutely the opposite of the theme developed in the quatrain as a whole—the theme of freedom, or independence.

Britain, America and France

•

Given that we have had such a clear statement about the Declaration of Independence, it is only reasonable for us to examine another American quatrain that deals with the future of the political promise contained in this document. Quatrain IV:96 offers a very succinct prophecy about how long democracy (or perhaps republicanism) will last in the United States.

CENTVRIE IIII.
XCVI

La fœur aifnee de l'ifle Britannique,
Quinze ans deuãt le frere aura naiffance:
Par fon promis moyennant verrifique,
Succedera au regne de balance.

The verse in the 1557 edition used here contains the curious *saeur*, and one abbreviation, and slight editorial amendments are included below to make it more suitable for modern readers.

La soeur aisnée de l'Isle Britannique,
Quinze ans devant le frere aura naissance:
Par son promis moyennant verrifique,
Succedera au regne de balance.[63]

It is difficult to say precisely what the French *moyennant verrifique* means—especially in relation to a promise—so this translation of the third line is less assured than usual. For the moment, we will not attempt to translate the word *Balance*, even though its meaning is crystal clear, in the arcane context within which Nostradamus worked.

The eldest sister of the British Isle,
Will have [her] birth fifteen years before the
        brother,
by his promise made under tested conditions,
[She] will continue to the reign of Balance.

Who is the eldest sister (*La soeur aisnée*) of the British Isle? Indeed, what is the British Isle? It would make sense that the British Isle is England, bearing in mind that it was the English parliament that lost the eldest sister—the main subject of this quatrain.

Let us presume that the eldest sister is the offspring of England—the United States. This was not only the first-born of British colonialism, but it is also visualized, almost always, in a feminine guise.

* * *

Historically speaking, the American colonies were the first signs of Empire that Britain established. The offspring of this foundation might therefore accurately be described as being "the oldest" (*aisnee*) children of this country. Equally, the colonies, under their new designation as the United States, were the first to mature and secede from British control.

If this line does indeed refer to the United States, then we have a very precise date. We could say that the United States was born in July 1776, with the Declaration of Independence (see page 59), which is the subject of another quatrain.

Now, according to the second line of the quatrain, this eldest sister (*la soeur aisnée*) is born 15 years before the brother (*le frere*).

Is it reasonable to interpret the "brother" as the other revolutionary country, at the end of the 18th century—which is, of course, France? Perhaps it is, especially since France did offer military and financial aid to the Americans when they rebelled against Britain.

It has been argued that, while the image of the United States as the eldest sister of Britain is reasonable, that of France as a "brother" is not. Whether Nostradamus intended the "brother" to be that of Britain, or of the United States, seems irrelevant. The sex is questionable because France—*La Belle France*—is almost always represented as being feminine.[64] However, it is likely that what Nostradamus is reaching for, in this context of the Revolution, is the word *brother* (*frere*) expressed within the concept of Fraternity, which was supposed to have been one of the guiding principles of the Revolution. It is surely no accident that the statue of the French Republic, designed by the Morice brothers for the center of Place de la Republique, is a female. The three bronze figures on the upper part of her socle represent Liberty, Equality and Fraternity, and are of different sexes: *Fraternity alone is a male.*

Let us assume, for the sake of continuing an analysis of the quatrain, that this brother of the quatrain *is* France. We must then ask what relevance the 15-year period has, in regard to this relationship.

Exactly 15 years (to the month), after the birth of the United States, which did away with British sovereignty in America, the French revolutionaries agreed on the formal dethronement of Louis XVI. This decision was made partly in consequence of the attempted flight of the king, and his arrest at Varennes, which I have dealt with. The Jacobins, who were the most revolutionary of the political groups in the France of 1791, regarded this botched attempt at flight as an act of treason. In consequence, on July 17, 1791, they drew up a petition addressed to the people. This they carried to the Champ-de-Mars, and laid it on what they called "The Altar of the Country," for signature. This petition successfully called for the dethronement of Louis XVI.

One immediate consequence of this petition was that opposing positions became more deeply entrenched. Those who still demanded the restoration of the king met at Pilnitz, in Saxony, on July 27, and there signed a treaty threatening invasion, if the king were not restored to the throne. For their part, the anti-monarchists took up arms, and on September 30, a new Legislative Assembly was formed, to replace the Constituent Assembly set up by the Revolutionaries.

In accordance with the rules of this Assembly, Lafayette, who had been commander of the National Guard, was dismissed. To show their respect for this great man, the city of Paris presented him with a statue of George Washington, and a sword forged from an iron bar of the destroyed Bastille. The metal of the old prison had been popular with the Revolutionaries: among the gifts sent by Lafayette to George Washington was one of the main keys of the Bastille. There is some argument as to which of the two keys, still preserved in the United States, is that given by Lafayette. The massive version on display in the museum of the George Washington Masonic Memorial, in Alexandria, Virginia is over a foot long. Another version is preserved in Mount Vernon.[65]

By a curious twist of fate, one of the two important statues of George Washington in Paris also includes a statue of Lafayette. This double group is the bronze designed by A. Bartholdi (already famous for his Statue of Liberty on Liberty Island), in 1895. It had been sculpted on the commission of Georges Pulitzer, and intended as a gift to the city of Paris.[66]

The reason why it was possible for Nostradamus to visualize the United States and France as being related by the blood ties of sisterhood and brotherhood lies in certain of the reforms of the Legislative Assembly. The basis of these reforms rested on the idea of the sovereignty of the people, on the brotherhood of man. In the American experiment in democracy, this sovereignty was tested, found good, and embraced into the political and social life of the nation. In France, the experiment in democracy failed. The remnants of the French court and the aristocratic privileged classes resisted the new democracy, with the result that their positions became entrenched. The people spawned demagogues, who stirred up further rebellion, and the immediate consequences of the new-found power were terrible. Louis XVI was imprisoned in August 1792, and his public statues were broken to pieces. On August 14 of that year, the new Municipality went to the Assembly to be sworn in; before it were carried three banners, each inscribed with a word: *Patrie, Liberté* and *Egalité*. In the following month, the Prussian army invaded France, and captured Longwy. Immediately, blood-lust broke out in Paris, and the massacre of all suspected royalists began. The assassins, wearing tricolored scarves around their waists, and a wheat-ear in their buttonholes, murdered over ten thousand people in Paris alone, within a three-day period.

In all the history of mankind, nothing more horrible and wantonly cruel has been left on record by a people pluming themselves on their politeness and civilization than the massacres of September, 1792.[67]

My purpose here is not to examine the sorry spectacle of what the French revolutionaries made of the democratic impulse, which was opened up for them. What is of importance—because it is clearly hinted at in the Nostradamus quatrain—is the contrast between the healthy birth of a maturing democracy in the United States, and that abortive birth in France.

What are we to make of the third line of the quatrain? Perhaps we should see it as a continuation of the second line, which deals with the brother, France.

This "brother" who is born 15 years later has been born under the constraints of a promise that was made under certain tested conditions. Nostradamus probably has in mind the heady promise of the revolutionaries of 1776. This promise, of power to the people, in the spirit of fraternal equality, was not met in France.

The last line contrasts this failure with the successful experiment in democracy in the United States. This final line is masterly in its own promise, for it insists that the experiment in the United States will last "as far as the reign of Balance." Now, the French word *balance* is the equivalent of Libra—the zodiacal sign of the balance, which we have already studied, in connection with Phaethon (see page 45).

Here we have a reference to the curious dating system that Nostradamus frequently uses in his quatrains. This system is based on the theory that seven planetary angels govern history, in a special sequence. We need not trouble ourselves unduly about this system, which, in European literature at least, goes back to the influential Abbot Trithemius, of the 15th century.

Trithemius outlined a system of angelic rulerships, in which seven Archangels were given dominion over specific periods of history. He called these angels Secundadeians, and claimed that each period over which they had rule lasted for exactly 354 years and 4 months. Trithemius provided a complete list of the sequence of angelic rules, from the creation of the World. However, the only ones we shall find ourselves interested in here are those covering the period for which Nostradamus issued his prophecies. This is the period ending in 1525, when Nostradamus was 22 years old, up to the year 2589 AD—well over half a millennium into our own future. Trithemius tabulated the rule of the angels of Mars, the Moon, Sun, Saturn and Venus, from 1525 to 2944 AD, as follows. This tabulation was the one familiar to Nostradamus.[68]

ANGEL	PLANET	PERIOD OF RULE
Samael	Mars	1171 to 1525 and 4 months
Gabriel	Moon	1525 to 1880 and 8 months
Michael	Sun	1880 to 2235
Ophiel	Saturn	2235 AD to 2589 AD
Anael	Venus	2589 AD to 2944 AD

Some authorities, who have studied this system of Trithemius, give the end of Gabriel's rule as 1881. Even without this correction, however, the end for the solar, or Michaelic rule, should be 2236, as the 12 months in this triple series add up to a further year. Similarly for the beginning and ending of the Venusian rule, a year should be added.

When Nostradamus mentions the *regne de balance*, he has in mind this angelic rulership of Venus, the ruler of Libra. The American civilization will continue until at least the beginning of that period, and perhaps beyond.

As the tabulation indicates, according to the Secundadeian sequence, the age *Anael*, or Venus, will begin about 2589 AD. What Nostradamus is predicting is that the benign democratic principle will continue in the United States until at least that year.

The notion that civilizations have a sort of "lifetime"—a period strictly governing their incubation, development and maturity—is not widely accepted by ordinary historians. However, historians of esoteric thought recognize that civilizations have a "lifetime" of about 800 years. One of the best-documented studies of this periodicity has shown that civilizations rarely last for more than half a dozen years beyond these eight centuries.[69]

If we extrapolate, from the Secundadeian rulerships, we find that Nostradamus seems to recognize the extent of this "lifetime" for the civilization supported by the United States. From 1776, when that civilization might reasonably be said to have first seen the light of day, to the beginning of the Venus period, in 2589, is 813 years.

The Two Rocks

•

Henry Roberts interpreted quatrain I.87—"a truly shattering prediction"—as a prophecy of a war between the United States and the Soviets (mentioned on page 6), along with an earthquake and fire in New York. This interpretation is utter nonsense.

As we shall see, the quatrain deals with a period during World War II. It is set in the Mediterranean, when the Allied forces were preparing to take Italy, then under the control of Mussolini.

In the 1577 edition of the quatrains that is used in this book, there is a rather obvious typographical error in the first word. The font of the second *n* is correct, but the compositor dropped it in upside down. It was an error picked up by editors in subsequent editions. For this reason, the original text appears opposite followed by the correct reading.

LXXXVII

Enuoſigée feu du centre de terre,
Fera trembler autour de cité neufue:
Deux grãs rochers lõg tẽs ferõt la guerre
Puis Arethuſa rougira nouueau fleuue.

The quatrain should read:

Ennosigée feu du center de terre,
Fera trembler autour de cité neufue:
Deux grands rochers long temps feront la guerre,
Puis Arethusa rougira nouveau fleuve.[70]

The analysis that follows will explain many of the more complex terminologies in this verse, but for the moment, we will use the following translation:

The thunderer Poseidon fire from the center of the
    earth,
Will make tremble the environs of the New City:
Two great rocks will make war for a long time,
Then Arethusa will redden (the waters) of a new
    river.

The opening word, *Ennosigée*, sets the theme of this startling quatrain. The word is a French version of the Greek name for Poseidon, the sea god, in his role as "Earth Shaker."[71] What does Nostradamus foresee as being subject to this terrible god, who has the power to shake the earth in such a way?

The location of the future event is revealed in the second line. We learn from this that the earth shaking, the fire from the center of the earth, will take place around the new city (*cité neufue*). Just as the name for

Poseidon is expressed in Greek, so is the identity of the new city. Nostradamus is writing of *Nea Polis*, which is the Greek for "New City"—the ancient name for Naples, in Italy.

It seems evident, then, that the quatrain deals with events relating to Naples, or its area. The reason why it is possible to identify the "new city" as Naples is not at all obscure: indeed, the identity was established in the 17th and 18th centuries by commentators on Nostradamus. What these early commentators failed to see was the *meaning* behind the quatrain—chiefly because the event predicted did not take place until the 20th century.

One anonymous commentator, aiming to criticize both the person and writings of Nostradamus, dismissed it as being nothing more than a *general* prediction. By this, he meant that the verse was about an event that was inevitable—just waiting to happen—and therefore required no special clairvoyant vision. After all the city of Naples had been built on the side of a volcano, and in an area well known for volcanic action; one day, Naples would surely be overwhelmed. He quoted a recent example, in that part of the world, when the Sicilian town of Catania was totally destroyed by the eruption of Mount Etna, in 1693.[72]

While this criticism might have seemed well founded at the time, in light of subsequent events the anonymous commentator was proved very wrong indeed. As we shall see, Nostradamus had a precise and very terrible event in mind, which certainly had something to do with earth shaking, but nothing to do with volcanoes. The deeper meaning of the quatrain must be sought, initially, in the third line. We must identify the two great rocks [*deux grās rochers*) that will make war for a long time.

It has been suggested that the two rocks point to the San Andreas Fault—the "two plates of rock in the earth's crust," which rub against each other and produce earthquakes. The tremors from this clash will be felt even in New York.[73] This reading seems to have been impelled by the insistence that the new city (*cité neufue*) was indeed New York, rather than Naples.

It has been suggested by more than one commentator that the two rocks are the Scylla and Charybdis of Greek mythology. As will be seen, I cannot agree with this reading. However, I do recognize that the mythology helps reveal the setting of the quatrain as being the Gulf of Messina, between the northeast tip of Sicily and Reggio on the mainland.

The sea monster named Scylla had once been a beautiful nymph, who was changed into monstrous form by the jealous witch, Circe. She was condemned to live on the rock of the same name, situated on the eastern side of the Straits of Messina. She is said to have had twelve feet and six heads, and to have barked like a dog. Nostradamus would have been familiar with the popular *Metamorphoses* of Ovid, in which Scylla is represented as a rock.

> *Scylla infests the coast to the right hand, while*
> *Charybdis holds the left. One grasps at passing*
> *ships,*
> *And sucks them down, only to spew them out.*
> *Scylla has raging dogs tethered to her hell black*
> *waist.*[74]

As these lines suggest, Charybdis is a whirlpool, off the coast of Sicily. Ships attempting to maneuver the Straits of Messina had to pass between the two dangers of this whirlpool and the crashing rock of Scylla. From this classical mythology derives the idea that, in attempting to avoid the rock of Scylla, one is sucked into the drowning waters of Charybdis. However, this interpretation requires some adjustment; Nostradamus mentions not one, but *two* rocks.

Of course, rocks do not make war. Is it possible that Nostradamus visualized a war between the two countries represented by the rocks? Or were these two the subject of a single invasion?

In fact, the only war that did seem to have the destructive violence that Nostradamus visualized was in relatively modern times, during World War II. The two allies (America and Britain) were ranged against the Axis powers—the combined forces of Italy (under Mussolini) and Germany (under Hitler).

Given the Sicilian setting, the line suggests two rocks in the vicinity of Sicily. Both appear to be shaken as though by an earthquake. For an understanding of this cryptic line, we must turn to events during World War II.[75]

The two rocks (*deux rocher*) are Pantelleria and Sicily. Prior to World War II, the Italians, under Mussolini, had fortified the island of Pantelleria. The Fascist press had become inordinately fond of this emblem of military power, and referred to it as their "Italian Gibraltar"—a reminder that the British called their own Gibraltar "the rock."[76]

The quatrain deals with the beginning of what has been called "one of the great campaigns in history"— the liberation of Europe from German military control.[77] It is generally believed that the first invasion of Europe by American and British troops was in July 1943, when Patton landed the American Seventh Army at Gela, and Montgomery landed the British Seventh Army between Pachino and Pozzallo, in the Gulf of Salerno. However, for this invasion to have been possible, the Allies would have had to capture from the Italians and Germans both Pantelleria and Sicily.

It was from the latter island that the invasion of the mainland, by 160,000 American and British troops, was mounted, in July.

The taking of these two islands marked the first steps in the invasion of Nazi-occupied Europe by American and British troops. No doubt this is one reason why Nostradamus elected to emphasize the importance of this terrible bombing of the two islands. Both were subjected to bombing of incredible intensity, such as would warrant Nostradamus likening the event to a vast earthquake, or volcanic action.

Pantelleria is a huge rock island, to the south of Sicily, with an area of just over 40 square miles. Believing it to be more heavily fortified than it really was, the American and British air forces mounted 5,285 attacks on the island, during which they dropped 6,200 tons of bombs, between May 8 and June 11, 1943. On one day alone, toward the end of this bombardment, over 1,500 tons were dropped. The demoralized Italians surrendered without resistance to the first seaborne attack.

Sicily itself—the second rock—was invaded by American and British amphibious troops on July 10, but for some days prior to this event the island was blasted by intensive bombing. After Sicily was wrested from the German occupiers, 1,100 aircraft were found destroyed on the airfields. Over half of these were German. To this figure should be added the 740 planes destroyed in the air. The city of Messina, on the northeastern tip of the island, was the main target of the bombing campaign. In the official reports relating to this campaign, there is one line that reminds us directly of Nostradamus's quatrain: after the bombing, the city was reduced to the condition in which it had been left by the terrible earthquake of 1909.[78] Although entire books have been written about the effects of bombing in such cities as Rome and Salerno, it was Messina that was the most heavily bombed of all Italian cities.[79]

On July 10, 160,000 Allied troops landed on the beaches of Sicily, with 350,000 to follow. The larger "rock," which we take to be Sicily, was subjected to the same intensive bombing before the seaborne attacks began. It was the largest military invasion in history. In the seaborne landings were 115,000 British empire troops, and over 66,000 American assault troops. It was officially recorded as the largest amphibious operation in history, before the massive operation Overlord, on the Normandy beaches.[80]

What are we to make of the final line in the quatrain? Who was Arethusa? And what had she to do with making the waters of a new river red?

The story of the mythological nymph's fruitless attempt to escape the river god Alpheus is told dramatically by Ovid, in his *Metamorphoses*.[81] The god's passions were raised when he saw Arethusa bathing in his waters. After he had pursued the naked nymph relentlessly, mile upon mile, she cried out in despair to Diana for help. In response, the goddess "cleft the earth," and Arethusa, now changed to water, was borne through blind caverns to reach Ortygia, once an island off Syracuse, in Sicily. Here she remained, as a sacred fountain.

This *Fonte Arethusa* is still preserved as a sacred site at Syracuse. In the popular imagination, it is believed to be connected by a water channel to the site of the river source, in Arcadia. The waters of this stream are said to flow from Arcardia, without mingling with the sea waters.

In view of what we have just seen about the destruction of Sicily, let us amend our initial translation of the final line, without dislodging any of the original French. In this case the line should read:

Puis Arethuse rougira nouveau fleuve.

Then the Fountain of Arethusa will redden (from) a new river.

Although there is a possibility that Nostradamus visited Italy, there is no evidence to show that he ever saw the Fountain of Arethusa.[82] However, her fountain in Ortyga was very famous in medieval times, and he would have been familiar with the story of the nymph from his reading of Ovid.

His reference to the fountain Arethusa making red a new river is explicable in terms of ancient Greek mythology. It was believed that the waters in the *Fonte Arethusa* at Syracuse would be stained red each year at the time of the annual sacrifice at Olympia. The rationale behind this mythology was that the river Alpheus, which runs to the south of the sacred site at Olympia, was stained red by the blood of the numerous sacrificial victims. In its unhindered course through the waters of the Mediterranean, this blood was carried as far as Syracuse.

There may be an element of irony behind Nostradamus's words. Perhaps he had in mind that, during the Olympic games, there was the proclamation of a three-month truce among all warring groups in the Mediterranean. In the Sicily of 1943, no such peace was possible, and Nostradamus seems to suggest that the fountain became red with blood as from another source. Perhaps Nostradamus was referring to a river of blood?

> *Then the Fountain of Arethusa will redden (from)*
> *a new River of blood.*

While this reading—or something very close to it—is a satisfactory interpretation of the quatrain, there are other, subsidiary, meanings in the line. When seeking for a meaning to the word *rougira*, we should recall that, often, Nostradamus will slip in a word derived from the language of the place he has mentioned in that particular verse. While the French verb *rougir* (*rougira* is third person future) certainly means "to redden" or "to paint red," the equivalent word in Italian has an entirely different meaning. The Italian verbs *rugghiare* and *ruggire* mean "to roar" (the noun is *il ruggito*). Such a verb could be taken as referring to the roar of battle, bombing and assault craft. Such a meaning completely transforms the significance of the second line. Did Nostradamus have in mind this bombing, when he described:

> *Fire, from the center of the earth,*
> *Will make the surrounds of Naples tremble.*

The Anglo-American attacks were successful, if bloody. The entire island was under the control of the Allies by August 17, 1943. One immediate consequence of this successful attack on Sicily is that the Italian people lost all heart for the fight. Mussolini was deposed, and was replaced by Pietro Badoglio, who put *il Duce* under arrest.

Meanwhile, the invasion of the Italian mainland by the Allies had begun. The new prime minister, Badoglio, undertook to stop fighting, and surrendered unconditionally to General Eisenhower. Unfortunately, Hitler, believing that it was essential to hold Italy, began to pour German troops into the country. The war was renewed, with disastrous consequences for Italy. The whole of Italy was turned into a war zone, and there were heavy losses on both sides. It was only after Bologna fell to the Allies, in April 1945, under the command of General Clark, that the Germans agreed to an unconditional surrender, and, on May 2, the Axis powers in Italy and western Austria laid down their arms.

However, what is of immediate relevance is that the invasion, mounted from Sicily, led to a stream of blood that linked the two rocks to the mainland.

The trembling of the earth, predicted in the second line of the quatrain, is echoed in the mythological account of the goddess he identifies by name in the fourth line. Accordingly, we will deal with this later, when examining the possible meaning of this obscure line. Is Nostradamus likening the pursuit and rape of Arethusa, the cleaving of the earth, and her escape to Sicily to the rape and destruction of Sicily and Italy during World War II? If this is the case, we must ask what this new river (*nouveau fleuve*) is, which Arethusa will redden (*rougira*). In Ovid's account, there is no indication that the stream into which she was turned, to make her escape, was red. Why should Nostradamus introduce this idea now? Perhaps he did this because he could foresee that, while Arethusa escaped, Italy did not. Because Hitler elected to fight on, the pursuit of victory, by the armies of the United States and Britain, certainly did redden Italian soil.

The mythological background to Arethusa's story does seem to be introduced because it links the mainland with Sicily, and also because it offers the imagery of a trail of blood. However, by a curious coincidence, a British cruiser, named *Arethusa*, was involved in naval operations in the Mediterranean.[83] The vessel was deployed mainly in convoy duties in the relief and support of Malta, to the south of Sicily, and, in discharge of these duties, traveled more than once the full length of the Mediterranean, between the Rock, Malta and Alexandria. In November 1942, she was damaged by an aerial torpedo, with the loss of 155 men. The *Arethusa* was, in fact, the last warship, operating in the relief and support of Malta, to be damaged by the enemy. But this is mentioned merely as a coincidence—it is impossible to think for one moment that Nostradamus had this vessel in mind when he elected to use Greek mythology as the basis for his verse.

The Settlement of Jamestown

•

As we have seen, quatrain II.54 was interpreted by Henry Roberts as predicting the iniquity of Pearl Habor, on December 7, 1941. It is utterly mystifying how Roberts could read this event into the words of Nostradamus. However, to exculpate Roberts to some extent, we should note that *his* version of the French quatrain contains ten errors, including two totally wrong words![84]

> *Par gent estrange, & Romains loingtaine*
> *Leur grand cité apres eaue fort troublée:*
> *Fille sans trop differente domaine,*
> *Prins chief, ferreure n'avoir esté riblée.*[85]

For the moment, let us translate this as:

> *By strange people, and distant Romans*
> *Their great city afterward by water much troubled:*
> *Young woman with too different a domain,*
> *The leader taken, the iron-worker not having been put in order.*

There are biblical overtones in the first line. The word *gent* suggests Gentiles, *Romains* suggests the letter to the Romans. We shall explore this biblical association shortly. The word *loingtaine* (which means "far distant") suggests that Nostradamus is writing of that distant land of the Americas, rather than about his favorite country, France.

As is often the case with Nostradamus's verses, the clue to the internal action and timing lies in the final line. In this quatrain, the line tells of a captured leader. This individual seems to have been an ironworker who was, in some unspecified way, not properly adjusted— perhaps not fit to be a leader.

To understand who this captured leader (*Prins chief*) is, we must first establish what the rest of the line means. As intimated in the English parallel, a *ferreure* is an ironworker, "one who fits with irons"—someone who, for example, shoes a horse. The verb *ribler* means "to dress stonework," or to true something up: that is, made to fit.[86] If we stick to the analogy of shoeing a horse, then the suggestion is that we have a reference here to someone who has shoed a horse without any great precision, or not in the ordinary way.

The identification proposed here for this person may appear strange at first, yet we shall see that the context of the verse makes sense in light of this proposal. It is possible that the line refers to John Smith, of the Jamestown settlement in early 17th-century Virginia. The English word *smith* does indeed suggest the metal-working *ferreure*, a man who works in metal. But why should Nostradamus describe John Smith as an inept *ferreure*, or as one who, somehow, did not fit the situation?

This must surely be a strange view of Smith. After all,

Smith was one of the most remarkable of all those remarkable men who colonized Virginia, in the early 17th century. His sense of adventure and his extraordinary energy made him an ideal leader for the pioneering enterprise: he was responsible for exploring tracts of the North American coast, and making surprisingly accurate maps, from Penobscot to Cape Cod. It was he who gave to North America the names *New England* and *Plymouth*, and he was probably the first Englishman to set eyes on the rough and boggy woodlands where the city of Washington, D.C. would eventually be built.

It is quite true to say that without Smith, it is unlikely that the original settlement in Jamestown, founded in 1607, would have survived. However, there are several reasons why anyone could regard Smith as a misfit of sorts—not least because he was constantly at loggerheads with his financiers in England. The London Company, which had set out the finances to support the colonization of Jamestown, was at loggerheads with Smith. The Company was seeking a quick profit on the initial outlay, and constantly criticized Smith for his seeming inability to send back good-quality cargoes. Smith, on the other hand, was interested in colonization, not in profits. He recognized that, before trade could become efficient, it would be necessary to establish enduring and healthy colonies. The conflicts between the London Company and Smith were never settled, and during 1609 the Company drew up a new charter, which effectively dismissed Smith from his job.

Perhaps it is this irreconcilable tension between the Company and Smith that Nostradamus had in mind when he wrote *ferreure n'avoir esté riblée*. The words could be read as meaning "Smith not having been brought into line."

But what about the first two words of the last line: the leader is captured (*Prins chief*)? Smith was a captured leader in more than one sense. In fact, the two words are ambiguous. They may be read as meaning either that the chief was captured, or that the chief did capture. Engravings from a work published by Smith himself, in 1624, show two events that seem to cover this ambiguity. The first (below) shows Smith capturing one chief (the king of Pamaunkee) in 1608.

The second picture (see facing page) shows Smith captured. He is just about to receive the blow from which he was saved by young Pocahontas. The text at the foot of this picture reads, "King Powhatan commands C. Smith to be slayne . . ."

Smith had an irascible personality, and was never

C. Smith taketh the King of Pamaunkee prisoner 1608

King Pothatan comando C. Smith to be flaine, his daughter Pokahoutas beggs his life has thankfulness and how he subiected 39 of their kings. reads history.

printed by James Bore

averse to throwing himself into dangerous situations in order to gain an advantage, and this helped to add events so extraordinary that his life suggests an adventure story more than an ordinary history. Even on his first sea voyage to Jamestown, he was arrested on a false charge of conspiracy. Since he was not, at that point, the leader of the band of colonists, perhaps it is not this arrest that Nostradamus had in mind. Later, after he had been made leader of the colonists, he was captured by Indians on more than one occasion. Early in 1608, at the instigation of his enemy, Gabriel Archer, Smith was arrested, tried for murder, and sentenced to be hanged. It was only the arrival of a supply ship from England, under Captain Newport, that saved Smith from the gallows.

Although there were several times during Smith's short time in Jamestown when he could have been described as "the leader captured," there is really only one *famous* captivity associated with Smith's life in the colony. In fact, Smith was a "captured leader" during one of the most famous events in North American history. In his personal accounts of his exploits, Smith tells us that, in December 1607, while searching for the source of the river Chickahominy, he was captured by Indians, and saved only by the intervention of the young princess, Pocahontas (illustration on page 87).

The story of Pocahontas is a delightful one, yet it was not told by Smith himself in his earliest detailed accounts of his experiences in North America. The first account of the Pocahontas rescue did not appear until 1624, in Smith's *Generall Historie of Virginia*. By this time, Pocahontas was famous in England, and had been fêted in London for some time—both as a royal Indian princess, and as the first Christian convert from her tribe. However, even if the story were not true in a historical sense, then it must be thought of as being true in a psychological sense. The princess herself was real enough—her bodily remains are still in a vault in Gravesend, near London. The blood from her veins still runs in later generations, in America. Indeed, the wife of President Woodrow Wilson could trace her ancestry back to the son born to Pocahontas and her English husband, John Rolfe, in 1617.

The opening words, *gent estrange*, seem to have a double meaning. The settlement of Virginia was undertaken among Indians, a foreign people (which is one meaning of *gent estrange*). On the other hand, Smith himself was a *gent estrange*, "a strange person."

Having made some sort of sense of the first and last

lines, let us examine the remaining two, to see if they have relevance to the Virginia undertaking.

Their great city (*Leur grand cité*) also has a double meaning. First of all, it has relevance to the London Company—an interpretation that lends emphasis to the possessive pronoun, *their* (*Leur*), for, technically and legally, the Company owned the settlement, lock, stock and barrel. Secondly, it refers to Jamestown itself. As suggested previously, Nostradamus frequently uses the word *grand* to describe important people. James I, after whom the town was named, was King—the grandest of all the grand in England, as his position in the center of the royal portraits at the head of Smith's book on Virginia indicates. Of course, in 1607—the year to which the quatrain refers—Jamestown was little more than a village, but Nostradamus was very accurate in his vision of futurity.

How are we to read "after water" (as we have interpreted *apres eaue*)? In fact, when used adverbally, *après* can mean "afterward." What is "afterward water," when applied to Jamestown? The words seem to point to important geographical changes that affected the history of the settlement. Jamestown in Virginia is now an island. However, when the settlers reached it in 1607, it was a peninsula, and it remained so until the 19th century. John Smith took advantage of this, for he was able to build a blockhouse on the land bridge, in order to be in a position to defend Jamestown with ease.[87]

Whether the remaining two words, *fort troublée*, refer to the waters or to the fortlike township is not clear, but in either case the prediction would be precise. The waters of the James River did "trouble" the peninsula so thoroughly that, by the 19th century, the land bridge was totally eroded. At the end of that century it proved necessary to build an extensive wall to stop further land erosion.

Deaths among the early settlers were numerous; by the time the first supply ship arrived, in January 1608, only 38 of the original 105 settlers were still alive. The winter of the next year (by which time John Smith had been removed from office by the London Company) was known as the "starving time." The township itself was also deeply troubled, and it is likely, since the original settlement was little more than a fort (giving his words, *fort troublée*, a double meaning), that this is what Nostradamus had in mind.

The settlement was first located on ground so marshy that it soon proved to be unhealthy. The buildings were also accidentally burned to the ground in 1609; although rebuilt, the town was virtually destroyed by Nathaniel Bacon in 1676. When the seat of the government of Virginia was moved from Jamestown to what is now Williamsburg, in 1699, the village was deserted, and became moribund. Fortunately, the old remains, which included the brick church and much of the graveyard, have been carefully restored, and a new brick church was built, designed to reproduce that finished by the settlers in 1647.

A shaft now marks the site of the original settlement. Monuments to Captain John Smith and Pocahontas have also been erected.

Given the setting and time—that is, Jamestown in 1607—the daughter (*Fille*) must be the daughter of King Powhatan, the princess Pocahontas. Perhaps, as a native Indian, she could be described as being "without a too different domain" (*sans trop differente domaine*) because she, unlike the settlers, was on her own land— literally, a native.

Earlier, it was suggested that one reason why Nostradamus introduced the quatrain, by establishing a link with the Apostle Paul's letter to the Romans, is because there was a religious theme behind the quatrain. This is true. The word *gent* (*Par gent*) suggests the word *Gentiles*, and, in the *Letter of Paul the Apostle to the Romans*, there is a very relevant verse that contains this word:

> For when the Gentiles, which have not the law, do by nature the things contained in the law, these, having not the law, are a law unto themselves:[88]

The verse seems eminently suitable for the religious life established by these settlers in Jamestown. It was here that the first truly Ánglican church was built, wherein the Protestants might worship according to their own law. There is no doubt that it was this that attracted Nostradamus to the romantic story of Jamestown and John Smith. However, there is another strain of meaning in this reading of the quatrain. The English who settled in Jamestown were the colonial forebears of those English who later decided (quite rightly, given the circumstances) to become a law unto themselves, and rebel against British intolerance.

Harnessing Electricity

•

We learned earlier in this book that Henry C. Roberts interpreted Quatrain II.91 as predicting the explosion of a nuclear device. Roberts claimed that the attack would come from the north, at sunset.

As we shall see, the quatrain actually deals with the practical exploitation of electricity, toward the end of the 19ᵗʰ century. Here follows a commentary in support of this reading.

A large number of the Nostradamus verses make use of cosmic phenomena as the guide to dating events within the verse. The fascinating quatrain II.91 is a particularly fine example of this, for the various predictive themes within its complex structure are woven together by cosmic imagery centering upon comets.

> *Soleil levant un grand feu on verra,*
> *Bruit & clarté vers Aquilon tendant.*
> *Dedans le rond mort & cris on orra,*
> *Par glaive, feu, faim, mort las attendas.*[89]

Tentatively, let us translate this as:

> [At the] rising of the Sun one will see a great fire,
> Noise and bright light holding toward the North.
> In the world, death, and one will hear cries,
> By blade, fire, hunger, death will attend them.

This is a typical construction. One line is given over to specifying a particular year, by which one may date the predicted events, which are themselves revealed in the remaining lines. The dating offered by the quatrain is hidden in the first line.

> *Soleil levant un grand feu on verra*

> [At the] rising of the Sun one will see a great fire,

What is this Sun rising (*Soleil levant*)? On a superficial level, we might dismiss it as a reference to an unspecified sunrise, but in so doing we would be missing something of great importance in the understanding of the Nostradamus quatrains.

The fact is that Nostradamus employed several methods of dating events. Among these methods was a system of time cycles set down in the late 15th century by the occultist Trithemius. We have already seen an example of this dating by the planetary angels, on page 70. Nostradamus was intimately familiar with this system, and demonstrated its working in a letter he wrote to the French king, Henri II, in 1557. Nostradamus employed this method of "angelic" dating in over 25 quatrains.

The dating system that Nostradamus borrowed from Trithemius was also discussed in connection with the relationships among Britain, France and the U.S., but perhaps it would be good to repeat it here, briefly, with reference to this particular quatrain.

Trithemius outlined a system of angelic rulerships, in which seven Archangels were said to rule specific periods of history. He claimed that each period over which they had rule lasted for exactly 354 years and 4 months. Trithemius provided a complete list of the sequence of angelic rules, from the beginning of the World, but the only three we shall find ourselves interested in are those covering the period during which Nostradamus lived, up to the year 2236 AD—well over two hundred years into our own future. The rule of the three angels of Mars, the Moon and Sun, from 1525 (when Nostradamus was 22 years old) to 2236, was tabulated by Trithemius in the following way. This was the tabulation familiar to Nostradamus.[90]

ANGEL	PLANET	PERIOD OF RULE
Samael	Mars	1171 to 1525 and 4 months
Gabriel	Moon	1525 to 1880 and 8 months
Michael	Sun	1880 to 2235

As mentioned earlier, some authorities who have studied Trithemius give the end of Gabriel's rule as 1881. Even without this correction, however, the end for the solar, or Michaelic rule, should be 2236, as the 12 months in this triple series add up to a further year.

It is only in reference to this arcane system of dating that we may make sense of the first line of this quatrain. In terms of the Planetary angels, the Age of the Sun began in 1880, or 1881. Michael, the angel of the

Sun, is usually portrayed with sunbeams around his head, carrying a golden sword suggestive of solar rays. In the engraving below, his whole face is portrayed in the form of a radiant sun.[91] The beginning of this solar age of Michael could rightly be described in terms of a sunrise.

How are we to read this phrase, the "rising of the Sun" (*Soleil levant*)? Is Nostradamus referring to the first flash of the Sun, when the solar body is still mainly hidden beneath the horizon, or is he referring to the moment when the orb of the Sun is completely separated from the horizon? We must ask the question only because the popular word, "sunrise" is not especially precise in meaning. Should we translate this imprecision into the Nostradamus quatrain?

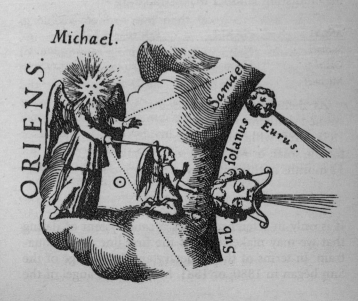

For instance, are we to take the reference to the sunrise as an identification of the years 1880 or 1881—or are we to allow a certain latitude? For example, should we take into account the years on either side of these two dates (symbolically speaking, the first flash, and the total separation), which is to say 1879 to 1882?

Was there any event in *any* of these years that would explain Nostradamus' prediction, expressed in the first line? Was there a great fire (*un grand feu on verra*) in evidence, between 1879 and 1882?

A "fire in the sky" is one dramatic, or poetic, way of describing a comet. Nostradamus had a number of different ways of referring to comets, for, in the days of naked-eye astronomy, their appearances were less common than in modern times. For this reason, they offered a useful method of dating events.[92]

There were no fewer than four comets visible in 1881, the most famous of which was Encke's comet, visible from Washington, D.C. during September of that year.[93] The comet seen in New South Wales, in May 1881, gradually became one of the most splendid cometary displays for several years. Its nucleus was as bright as a star of the first magnitude, and its fiery tail was 20 degrees long. It remained visible to the naked eye for almost five months. It was rivaled only by the magnificent comet of 1861, which was almost as bright as Venus, and could be seen even at noon. Its 100-degree arc left a strange glow in the sky, and contemporaneous scientists calculated that it was moving at 10 million miles per day: it was rightly called the Great Comet.[94]

It is, of course, impossible for us to determine, now, which of the comets of 1881 Nostradamus had in mind.

Indeed, it is quite possible that he had all four in mind. However, the greatest of the comets was first seen in Gemini. This, to a medieval astrologer, would explain entirely the last part of the quatrain, for in the medieval astrological tradition, a comet appearing in this sign would bring wars (*glaive, feu*) and famine (*faim*).[95]

However, before examining in depth the latter half of the quatrain, let us look more closely at the comets, and other cosmic phenomena of that period.

The chemist and photographer Henry Draper, working at New York University, photographed the comet in Gemini—the first successful attempt to make such a record. Draper (and his father, John William Draper) made enormous advances in stellar photography. His father had taken the first photographs of the Moon, in 1840, and was the first to succeed in making a spectrum photograph of the Sun, in 1843. In fact, Henry Draper was the first photographer to make a successful picture of a star's spectrum—that of Vega, in 1872.

The assumption that Nostradamus is writing about a comet, or comets, that appeared in or around 1881 may be challenged (though the date itself is beyond doubt). There was another cosmic event, in 1880, which seems to have been just as relevant to the Nostradamus quatrain, and which is linked with yet another achievement of Henry Draper. In September 1880, working from Hastings-upon-Hudson, Draper photographed the Orion nebula, the *theta* of the constellation Orion. This nebula is only faintly visible to the naked eye. While it was certainly known to early 17th-century astronomers, there is no evidence that it had been noted or cataloged during the lifetime of Nostradamus.[96]

Orion is the name of the cosmic Warrior. In *Hecuba*, a play by the Greek Euripides, are descriptions of this constellation. It is portrayed alongside *Canis Major*, the Greater Dog, and both are visualized as ejecting flaming darts from their eyes:

> *Where Orion and the Greater Dog dart from their*
> *   eyes*
> *The flaming rays of fire.*[97]

Is this the origin of Nostradamus's second line, which predicts the noise & bright light toward Aquilon (*Bruit & clarté vers Aquilon*)? Certainly, this Greek source explains the reference to noise (*bruit*), for the Greater Dog is visualized in many early astronomical texts as barking, and disturbing the peace of the skies. In fact, in one quatrain, Nostradamus himself referred to the Greater Dog, howling all night.[98] This explanation, that the quatrain relates to the nebula in Orion, does help explain Nostradamus's use of the word *Bruit* in a way that a comet alone does not.

In effect, I am proposing that Nostradamus is referring to either the comets of 1881 or to the nebula in the constellation of Orion, which (presumably) he foresaw would be photographed in that same year. Either way, both of these cosmic events point securely to the years 1880 or 1881.

Nostradamus is scarcely ever vague when dating events, yet, in this case, we seem to have a period of two, or even three years, in which to search for a relevant prediction. Were there any events between, say, 1879 and 1882 that might be regarded as the fulfilment of the prophecy in the remaining three lines of the verse? An answer to this question requires us to look at the meaning of the second line from a different standpoint.

The third line describes noise and bright light (*Bruit & clarté*) holding toward Aquilon (*vers Aquilon tendant:*). Now, it is quite possible to read *vers Aquilon* as meaning "toward the north," but, on a number of occasions Nostradamus used a similar phrase to denote North America. Was there any event—perhaps in the States—falling between 1879 and 1882, which could be described in terms of noise and bright light?

There were, during this period, a bewildering number of events that make sense of this prediction, all of them being linked, in definite ways, with the practical use of the newfangled electricity.

In 1879, Dugald Clark used an electric arc to heat a steel furnace. In the same year, Siemens, in Berlin, exhibited the first electric railway. In Scotland, Crompton lit St. Enoch's Railway Station, by means of electricity, and in Berlin, at the Trade Exhibition, there was a demonstration of the first electric tram. In 1880, Thomas Edison, in the United States, and Joseph Swan in England, quite independently, made the first practical electric light. In 1882, Edison's generating station opened in Pearl Street, New York, to serve downtown Manhattan; one immediate consequence of this was the first street lighting by electricity in the city of New York. In the same year, the first hydroelectric plant was established at Appleton, Wisconsin.[99]

There could be no more precisely phrased three-word description of electric lighting than Nostradamus's *Bruit & clarté* . . . for surely it is possible to read *Bruit* as a reference to the noisy generators, and *clarté* as an indication of their end product?

What are we to make of the last two lines of the quatrain? These seem to have nothing to do with the benefits derived from the practical application of electricity, which dominated the four-year period covered by the first two lines.

> *Dedans le rond mort & cris on orra,*
>
> *In the world, death, and one will hear cries,*

Dedans le rond could be translated as "in the remaining part of the world."[100] The rotundity of the earth is being contrasted with the formlessness of space, in which the fire of the comet burns. It is a term relevant to the imagery of comets, for the visibility of these visitants is conditioned by their visibility in the north and south hemispheres. This is an important distinction, as the majority of discoveries and applications we have discussed so far originated in the United States. The reference to *le rond* (which has a different meaning from the feminine, *la ronde*) would suggest that Nostradamus is now turning his attention to events in the rest of the world, during this halcyon period of American expansion.

What Nostradamus foresaw for the rest of the world, during the period of expansion in the United States, seems to have been far from pleasant. The third line, after referring to the world at large, predicts death and cries; the fourth line is slightly more specific, but no less unpleasant.

> *Par glaive, feu, faim, mort las attendas.*
>
> *By blade, fire, hunger, death will attend them.*

Threatened are sword fire, hunger and death (*glaive, feu, faim, mort*). With the assumption that Nostradamus does have in mind the rest of the world—the globe in general—let us take the predicted events word by word. *Glaive* means sword, and *feu* means fire. Together, the words may be taken as a standard Nostradamian reference to war. In January 1879, the Zulus massacred British troops at Isandhlwana, Zululand, leading to the Zulu War. The Zulus were defeated at Rorke's Drift and Ulundi. The Boers revolted, and defeated the British in 1881, at Majuba.

In October 1879, Britain invaded Afghanistan, mainly in a response to the massacre of the British legation at Kabul, in the previous September. British forces were defeated at Maiwand, but General Roberts marched from the city of Kabul to Kandahar to depose the Khan, and replace him with a pro-British ruler.

In September 1881, there was a Nationalist rising in Egypt, under Arabi Pasha, against the British. By September 1882, Garnet Wolseley had defeated the Egyptians in Lower Egypt, and shortly afterward occupied the entire country and the Sudan.

Faim means hunger or famine. During the entire period of four years, one of the recurrent Irish famines raged. Early in 1880, considerable funds designed to relieve the famine arrived from the United States, Canada, Australia, and (surprisingly) from India, which had its own famine in that year. Although, in March and August 1880, the British Parliament dispensed relief funds in Ireland, it took a long time for the relief to become effective—partly because the year saw no fewer than 10,000 evictions from the land.[101]

Almost as though following the stellar symbolism of

Nostradamus, the U.S. ship *Constellation* arrived in Cork (Ireland), on April 20, carrying relief for what was by now called "Irish Distress."

Terrible as the Irish distress was, there were even worse famines during this period, in other parts of the *rond*. In China, over nine million people had died of hunger in 1878 alone, and this famine persisted well into 1880. A terrible famine hit Kashmir in 1879, caused mainly by unusual weather conditions during the previous years. The famines that decimated Asia Minor in 1880 were among the worst on record for the area. In fact, Nostradamus's single word *faim* points to a major instability in the world during the period under review!

One would think that, given the above notes, there is no need to read further into the significance of the word *mort*, which, of course, means death. Death did accompany (*mort las attendans*) the sword, fire and hunger. However, it is worth asking why Nostradamus should have used such curious "French" at this point of the quatrain.

The three words *mort las attendans* read more as Spanish than French.[102] Why would Nostradamus make this reference to Spanish death, in the 1879–81 period?

Perhaps Nostradamus was hinting at Spanish history of the period in order to point to an event in the United States.

On the last day of December 1879, Francisco Otero y Gonzalez attempted the assassination of the king and queen of Spain, by shooting them. Although the attempt failed, Otera was executed in April 1880. We can be reasonably sure that Nostradamus turned his last words of the quatrain into Spanish to reflect upon the execution of Otera. However, Nostradamus was not writing about this failed assassination and execution in a void.

It was well known, in astrological circles, that the appearance of a comet was a harbinger of the fall and death of great ones. This idea is so ancient that it may be traced back to the second century AD, in the writings of Ptolemy.[103] The comets' hidden power, to bring about earthquakes and the deaths of *grands*, was beyond dispute in ancient times. Astrologers often point out that when Halley's magnificent comet appeared in 1759, the event was followed by the death of George II. In the year of its appearance, terrible earthquakes were felt over an area of 10,000 square miles, touching upon Tripoli and Syria. The same comet became visible again, by means of the naked eye, in 1910: twelve days later, King Edward VII died.[104]

The comet, which appeared in June 1881, was described in an official report by Spencer F. Baird, the Secretary of the Smithsonian. He noted that the comet would return only once every 3,000 years.[105] Within weeks, the president of the United States of America, James Abram Garfield, had been shot in Washington, D.C. in July 1881. He did not die until September of that year. As mentioned previously, Encke's comet was visible from Washington, D.C. during September, 1881.

What *did* Nostradamus have in mind for one or the other of the comets of 1881, if it were not the assassination of Garfield, the much-loved president of the United States? Had not Nostradamus introduced the Spanish reference, it is unlikely that we would have been led to the idea of a presidential assassination at all.

* * *

Now that we have stripped out the several interwoven strands of meaning within the quatrain, let us look a little more deeply at some of the words that Nostradamus used with a precision that borders on genius.

The word *Aquilon*, in the second line, should be taken as referring to the United States. While the prophecy, on the whole, does relate in its broadest aspects to the history of the States, in this case *Aquilon* may have a different meaning. Ultimately, the word is linked with the watery *aquilus*, the rain-bringing wind that sweeps down from the north. But because it meant north, it was also used to denote the northern of the pair of fishes that denote the constellation Pisces. *Aquilonius*, or *Aquilonaris*, was the northern fish. The sign Pisces (which is, of course, a different thing from the constellation Pisces) is marked in the calendar by March: on March 21, the Sun moves into the next sign, Aries. It was while the Sun was in Pisces, on March 4, that Garfield was elected to the presidency.

Look carefully at the second line:

Bruit & clarté vers Aquilon tendant.

Bruit & clarté VERS AQUIlon tendant.

Do we overestimate the genius of Nostradamus if we interpret the two words *vers Aquilon* as relating to the zodiacal sign Aquarius? The secret of this Green Language encoding lies in the fact that *Verseau* is the French for Aquarius. Here, in this line, we have the first part of the word *vers* ranged against *Aqui*[lon]. Now, *aqua* is the Latin for water, which in French is *eau*. Hence, in terms of the rules of the Green Language, the structure may be read as *Vers-eau*, or *Aquarius*. Why would Nostradamus go to such lengths to hide the word *Aquarius* in his verse? Almost certainly, he did this because of the tradition associated with comets which are first seen with the naked eye, streaming through Aquarius.

In the days when princes were a fact of life, such an Aquarian comet would portend the death of some eminent prince, or, as Nostradamus would often put it, a *grand*. Substitute for prince such a word as president, and Nostradamus's meaning is clear. The comet of 1881 was to portend the death of the *grand* of the Aquilon—the president of the United States.

We see then, that in one occulted reference, Nostradamus points to the month in which President Garfield would be elected. He then points, in a similar occulted reference, to the manner of his death.

There remains one other important question raised by this quatrain. As indicated before, the second line of the verse touches upon the development of electrical power in the United States, and in the world at large. Why should Nostradamus link his future comet with electricity? The truth is that even the great Halley, whose name in the popular imagination is so closely linked with comets, believed that the tails of comets were composed of an "electric fluid." This term, *electric fluid*, would appear to have little meaning today, yet it may be traced back to the most esoteric of all secrets of the old alchemists.

Early Settlement of Florida

•

A prophecy made in 1562 is mentioned (see page 16) concerning an event that took place during the early exploration of the coasts of Florida, by the French. Nostradamus did not predict this event in his regular series of *Prophétie* quatrains, but in a predictive verse he wrote especially for the year 1562.

In order to appreciate fully the background to this verse, we shall have to glance at certain details of history. Writing in 1569, the medical doctor Cornelius Gemma tells a story of an astrologer who, eight years earlier, had made a lucky forecast of a future event. This gained for the astrologer such a reputation that Gemma reported, "if this prophet were to predict that the stars were about to fall from the skies, people would believe him." Gemma tells us that this astrologer is now dead, yet prognostications were still being published under his name.

The story, as told by Cornelius Gemma, fits Nostradamus perfectly. The year the prediction was made (1561), also fits Nostradamus perfectly.[106]

By 1569, when Gemma told the story of the famous astrologer, Nostradamus had been dead for three years. Gemma, like just about everyone of that time, believed that Nostradamus arrived at his prophecies by means of astrology. In spite of his demise, in 1569 the prognostications of Nostradamus were *still* being published. Not only would the *Prophéties* continue to be published for the next four and a half centuries, but some almanac makers had climbed onto the bandwagon. They were already putting out *Almanacs* and prophecies bearing the Seer's influential name, as though he were still writing from beyond the grave.[107]

In view of this, we cannot help but believe that Gemma's story is being told of Nostradamus. This view is supported by the prophecy itself, for one of his extraordinary predictive verses fits the story exactly. This quatrain was published in Nostradamus's *Almanach* for 1562, which he dedicated to Pius IV.[108] Although written in 1561, the verses in it were intended to deal with future events that would unfold in the following year.[109]

There were 13 gnomic verses in the almanac. Nostradamus had constructed one for the year in general (*Quatrain de l'An universel*, as the title page put it), along with 12 for each of the months, in named sequence. One of the delights of the almanac prophecies is that, in seeking to work out their meanings, one has no need to decode dates within the verses; the month and year are actually stipulated at the head of each quatrain.

In this particular series is a verse that deals with an

event that was to occur in 1562. When it *did* occur, it became famous throughout England, France and Spain. The verse headed April 1562 reads:

> *De LOIN viendra susciter pour mouvoir,*
> *Vain decouvert contre peuple infini,*
> *De nul congneu le mal pour le devoir,*
> *En la cuisine trouvé mort & fini.*[110]

It is by no means an easy verse to translate, especially as at least two of the verbs are no longer used in their 16th-century sense. Since we are interested only in what a 16th-century reader would have immediately perceived from the lines, let us deal only with one phrase and the last line.

In using the phrase *peuple infini*, Nostradamus seems to have in mind people in distant countries. This would correspond to the LOIN ("far") of the first line. However, it is the final line that would have caught the attention of the 16th-century reader, in light of events linked with April 1562.

Bearing in mind that the word *cuisine* can mean "kitchen," "cooked food," or even, in a general sense, "menu," this line may be translated approximately as:

> *In the food found dead and done with.*

It might also read,

> *In the cuisine, found dead and done with.*

As this verse for April 1562 suggests, even though one does not have to trouble oneself with deciphering dates, it is no more easy to understand the almanac verses of Nostradamus than the quatrains in his *Prophéties*. However, the translated line above offers a reasonable basis upon which to examine the meaning of the prediction, in relation to the events that transpired in this month of 1562.

The future events set out in this strange verse unfolded in a most dramatic way. In April 1562, two French ships reached the Florida coast, and cast anchor in what is now St. Augustine.[111] The ships had been sent from France by the admiral Gaspard de Coligny, the leader of the French Huguenots. They had come a long way (*De LOIN viendra*), for this was one of the longest and most dangerous sea voyages possible in those days. The Admiral, Coligny, hoped to establish in Florida a territorial and religious challenge to the Spanish enemy, who had already claimed most of the known lands of the Americas.

After anchoring off St. Augustine, a number of crewmen rowed to the shore, where they were received, in a friendly manner, by "a good numbre of the Indians, inhabytants there . . . all naked and of a goodly stature . . . very gentill, curtious and of a good nature."[112] These, I must presume, are the *peuple infini*, mentioned by Nostradamus in the second line of his quatrain (see page 108). The French sailors explored this "incomperable lande" for two weeks, and then, their mission of claiming it for France completed, prepared to return home. Before leaving, they constructed a fort on Parris Island, and named it Charlesfort, in honor of Charles IX of France. This rude fortification became famous in Europe, when it was included among the finest series of early engravings relating to Florida ever to be published (see page 110).[113]

Before sailing back to France, their captain, Jean

Ribault, arranged for 30 volunteers to remain behind. These were to await the return, in six months time, of more French ships, with provisions and additional men.

Things did not go well for those left behind. The fort was accidentally burned down, and starvation gripped them. At length, when it was evident that the promised relief would not come from France, they mutinied, built a small ship, and set out on the long voyage back home. Even the wind did not favor them. From time to time, they were driven back, and because of the delays, they ran out of food. They ate their shoes and leather jerkins. Then stormy weather damaged and threatened to capsize the vessel. Eventually, maddened with hunger, they killed one of their number, and ate his body. This is probably what Nostradamus had in mind when he wrote of *la cuisine* that found death and the end.

The full brilliance of Nostradamus's vision of futurity is revealed when we learn the name of the unfortunate who was eaten in this way. His name was La Chere—a homonym of the French word *la chair*, "flesh." The *cuisine* to which he referred was human flesh.

After more maladventures, the survivors were rescued by an English ship, and, while some were put ashore at Corunna, others were taken to England, where the failed French attempt at the settlement of Florida (*Vain decouvert*) soon became famous. While the final line of the verse has now taken on a gruesome meaning, the contemporaries of Nostradamus would have had no difficulty in understanding it, in light of events.

Therefore it is likely that it is this prediction that Cornelius Gemma had in mind, when he wrote about the famous astrological prophecy of 1562. The story of the terrible experiences of the survivors from Charlesfort became well known in England, France and Spain. In fact, the tale became so famous in England that Queen Elizabeth herself took an interest in it, with the result that several of the survivors were personally introduced to her. The French and Spanish had also learned about the story, mainly because the defection of the leader of the expedition, Ribault (still anxious to return to the men he had left behind in Florida), almost caused a diplomatic incident.

In 1564, during a temporary peace in the French civil war, a second sea voyage set out from France for Florida. However, by now, Ribault languished in an

English prison.[114] There can be no other "astrological" prediction relating to the year 1562 that could have been quite so famous as that which Nostradamus made for April of that year.

Pitt and St. Louis

•

Quatrain X.56 is a fine example of how Nostradamus could encode personal names that did not exist in his own day (see page 21). The following analysis of the quatrain reveals how he did this to encode both the name of a British politician and the name of an American city. The verse, in French, runs:

Prelat royal son baissant trop tiré,
Grand flux de sang sortira par sa bouche,
Le regne Anglicque par regne respiré,
Long temps mort vif en Tunis comme souche.[115]

The quatrain offers several challenges to translators, among which the most difficult are *Anglicque*, in the third line, and the phrase *mort vif*, and its related word *souche*, in the last line. At this point we will not attempt a translation of *Anglicque*, so for the moment, let us use the following for the verse as a whole.

Royal prelate his lowering carried too far,
A great flow of blood will pour from his mouth,

The royal Anglicque *will breathe with the royal,*
The long-time dead alive in Tunis as roots.

Quatrain X.56 is one of the more intriguing of the
Nostradamus predictive verses. It is intriguing mainly
because of the sophistication of its encoding, as well as
because of its subtle play on names and obscure words.
The clue that it has "American" overtones is initially
suggested by the word *Anglicque*, in the third line. This
word was used by Nostradamus in a number of verses
(albeit with a different spelling) dealing with American
themes.

A clue to the identity of the main participant in this
quatrain is to be had from the curious description in
the last part of the first line. Nostradamus tells us that
this individual takes his descent, or lowering (*baissant*),
too far, or too deep. This image suggests a hole in the
ground, or a deep pit. In turn, this suggests the name
Pitt.

Let us assume that Nostradamus had in mind the
18th-century English politician William Pitt the Elder.

We might confirm this assumption as being reasonable if we can show the relevance of the remaining description in the line. Is it possible that Pitt was
somehow a "royal prelate" (*prelat royal*)?

The word *prelate*, which is most frequently used in
an ecclesiastical context, is from the Latin *praelatus*, a
participle of *praeferre*—to be carried first, or in front.
This word does have a direct and almost unique relevance to Pitt. In 1766, on the command of George III,
William Pitt was made *first* Earl of Chatham. By *royal*
command he was put in a position where he could be
addressed by all as "the first." This royal appointment
explains why Nostradamus should have contrasted the

idea of abasement (the image *of baissant trop tiré*) with the high dignity of the *Prelat royal*.

This phrase, *Prelate royal*, is actually yet another sign of the genius of Nostradamus, as it puts a finger on one of the most important events for Pitt—one that had important ramifications in his life. George III made Pitt a peer of the realm in 1766, in exchange for a promise, made by Pitt, that he would attempt to form a stable government. His contemporary ministers were outraged at this elevation of a commoner, and the people were dismayed—almost as though they had lost a popular leader. It seemed to the populace that Pitt had joined the corrupt office-seekers, who were prepared to put their own interests before those of the public. He had been trusted as one who represented the genius of England, and now he had betrayed the trust, in the manner of a turncoat, changing from commoner Pitt to the aristocratic Earl of Chatham. "Pitt was adored— but Chatham's quite unknown," as one newspaper put it, expressing the views of a multitude.[116] It is true to say that after his elevation to the peerage, Pitt's political life changed, and with it his reputation. The two words used by Nostradamus seem almost to be a result of an intimate awareness of Pitt's personal history.

A great flow of blood will pour from his mouth,

How can we make sense of the link that Nostradamus seems to draw between William Pitt, and the somewhat distasteful idea of a stream of blood (*Grand flux de sang*) emerging from his mouth (*par sa bouche*)?

Just as the English *mouth* can refer to the mouth of the cannon, or the muzzle of a gun, so does the French *bouche*. While Pitt did not kill anyone directly, it was his speeches (the thing that came out of his mouth) that helped direct the course of the bloody Seven Years War that convulsed Europe and North America in the 18th century. He was, in a sense, responsible for much of this bloodshed.

The Seven Years War is the name given to a period of warfare fought initially in Europe, but which, because of the enmity between England and France, spread to North America. In the war, a coalition of France, Austria, Russia, Sweden and Saxony attempted to stop the encroachment of Frederick the Great of Prussia. Initially Britain offered subsidies to Frederick, and fought only against France. Britain, under the wise guardianship of William Pitt, was immensely successful in its campaigns in North America. Here, the bitter conflict with France resulted in vast territorial gains for Britain, mainly in Canada.[117] By the end of the Seven Years War, Britain was the most powerful colonial nation on earth. It is this moment of power, and the consequent fall from this pinnacle, that Nostradamus seems to have had in mind when he wrote the quatrain.

The reference made by Nostradamus to the flow of blood (*flux de sang*) was very relevant. The war had proved to be costly in terms of finance and men. When King George III, anxious for peace in Europe, made a speech in Parliament in 1759, he said that it was his heart's desire to put an end to *the effusion of Christian blood*.[118] At that time, however, the War had run only half its course.

The Seven Years War has been called Pitt's War. Indeed, it gained this name even while the conflict still raged.[119] It was William Pitt's genius as war minister that allowed Britain to achieve so much during the Seven Years War. Indeed, it was to Pitt, more than to any other individual, that Britain owed the acquisition of Canada, for it was his foresight, planning and willingness to take risks that led to such victories as that gained by General Wolfe on the Heights of Abraham, and the taking of Quebec.

Recognition of Pitt's achievements in the war came during his own lifetime. In 1758, General Forbes had captured from the French Fort Duquesne (the scene of Braddock's death, and George Washington's heroism). On taking the destroyed fort, Forbes effaced all French records, by naming it Pitt's Bourgh, after William Pitt, whom he recognized as the moving genius behind the British participation in the Seven Years War. The city that developed on this site, now called Pittsburgh, is a major city of Pennsylvania.

There is every good reason why Pitt should be regarded warmly by Americans. Pitt was more distressed than any other British politician at the threatened breach with the American colonies. In Parliament—literally to the very last—he argued that the colonists "freedom-loving sons of freedom-loving fathers" were right to feel threatened by the taxations imposed upon them by the British.[120] Throughout his parliamentary life, and his life in the Lords, he argued for friendly reconciliation with the colonies, and openly suggested that their position was not fully appreciated by the British government. He watched with horror as the British government sleepwalked into a war that with his profound knowledge of warfare, he recognized Britain could never win.[121]

La regne Anglicque par regne respire.

The royal Anglicque *will breathe with the royal,*

This enigmatic line is difficult to translate, and even more difficult to understand. After much thought, I have come to the conclusion that Nostradamus is drawing a parallel between a ship named after the English king (*regne Anglicque*) and his own reign (the second *regne* of the line). The two are seen as "breathing" together. The ship in question is that which was once the pride of the British navy, the *Royal George*.

The *Royal George*, launched in 1756, was a result of an effort made to improve the quality of warships in the British navy. She was 178 feet in length, and over 2,000 tons, with a crew of 750 men, and a display of 100 guns. Nostradamus refers to the ship because its superb warlike qualities corresponded to the superb warlike qualities of the British armies during the Seven Years War, while under the dominion of William Pitt.

In 1782 the *Royal George* was among the ships ordered to undergo a refit at Portsmouth, prior to sailing to relieve Gibraltar. In order to repair a leak, weights were shifted on the *Royal George*, and some rotted planking on her bottom fell out. She sank, with the loss of 800 men, including Richard Kempenfelt, the British rear admiral.

Nostradamus is linking the loss of this royal-named vessel with the loss of the colonies.

The Seven Years War had begun in 1756—the same year in which the *Royal George* was launched. The American colonies were finally lost in 1782, when the *Royal George* was sunk. This explains the significance of the third line, for the *reign Anglicque*, which we read as a reference to America under the British, breathed (*respiré*) its last in the same year as the other "reign"— the *Royal George*.

In 1782, England finally acknowledged the loss of America. The loss had become inevitable when Cornwallis surrendered to George Washington at Yorktown, in the previous year. The irony is that Nostradamus was pointing to the great contradiction of political expansion under George III. On the one hand, through the adroit handling of the Seven Years War, by William Pitt the Elder, Britain gained Canada. On the other hand, by the maladroit political handling of the American situation, Britain lost its most important colonial asset.

Is there any other reference in the quatrain that points to American history? As we have seen, in the first two lines of the verse, Nostradamus played with the name of Pitt. In the third line, he played with the name of the ill-fated *Royal George*, as a symbol of the loss of the colonies. It is therefore not surprising that, in the same verse, he should play with yet another name.

This name is contained in the final, deeply enigmatic line of the quatrain. This is indeed perhaps the most enigmatic of all the many lines that Nostradamus wrote.

Long temps mort vif en Tunis comme souche

The long-time dead alive in Tunis as roots.

Before we can begin to understand the meaning of this line, we must hazard a guess as to whom the "living dead" (*mort vif*) might be. The phrase suggests yet another Nostradamian quotation from the Bible. In *Isaiah*, we find the startling phrase:

Thy dead men shall live . . . [122]

For once, however, Nostradamus is not harking back to holy writ. The identity of this living dead man is found hidden in the last word of the fourth line. This French word, *souche*, has wrongly being translated as meaning "log," and has misled a number of Nostradamians who have no knowledge of French.[123] The word really means the lower part of the tree, including the roots. Because of this, *souche* has a secondary meaning of "roots," in the sense of "ancestral roots." We shall see that the final line of the quatrain is dealing with ancestral roots. Typical of the Francophile Nostradamus, these are the ancestral roots of a French king.

As we examine the line more closely, we shall discover that the ancestor of this king is the dead man, while the king himself was still alive, at the time when the prediction was being enacted, or fulfilled.

The dead (*mort*) "ancestor" to whom Nostradamus refers is St. Louis, the much-loved crusading French king, who was killed at the siege of Tunis, in 1270.

The living (*vif*) king was his namesake, Louis XV of France.

In 1764, Auguste Chouteau, and a group of workmen under his control, formed the first settlement at what was, within the year, to be called St. Louis. The name was bestowed on the settlement in honor of the reigning Louis XV, whose patron saint was St. Louis, who (as

Nostradamus reminds us) had died at Tunis. Thus, this city, which is now the most important in Missouri, was named after a living (*vif*) and a dead (*mort*) of the same name. The enigmatic *mort vif*, or living dead, is now explicable: St. Louis was named after a dead man, in honor of a living man.

The First Submarine

•

Quatrain III:13 affords an excellent example of the precision with which Nostradamus works, when dating events by means of astrological or astronomical phenomena. The verse opens with a line that may be understood only in terms of cosmic data:

> *Par fouldre en l'arche or, & argent fondu,*
> *Des deux captifz l'un l'autre mangera,*
> *De la cité le plus grand estendu,*
> *Quand submergee la classe nagera.*[124]

For the moment, we can translate this as meaning:

> *By lightning in the arc, gold and silver fused,*
> *The two captives will devour one another,*
> *Of the most grand city extended,*
> *When submerged the ship will swim.*

The first line opens explosively. *Par fouldre* is a 16th-century version of the modern French, *par foudre,* meaning, "by lightning," or "by means of a thunderbolt." In the verses of Nostradamus, it can also mean "an explosion." As we shall soon discover, the quatrain deals with an explosion that played an important role in American history.

In order to discover what *did* explode, we shall have to turn to the last line of the verse. Considering that he was describing an invention that did not really become operative until the late 18th century, Nostradamus could scarcely have been more specific than he was in this last line.

> *Quand submergee la classe nagera.*

> *When submerged the ship will swim.*

Classe is from the Latin *classis*, which means both "an army" and "a troop of men at sea"—that is "a fleet of ships." Nostradamus often uses the word to denote a single ship, filled with men.

Later versions of the *Prophéties* (than the 1557 edition quoted here) tend to add the necessary acute accent on *submergée*. This last word is in the singular, which means that we are dealing with one vessel. Since this ship is submerged, we might presume that Nostradamus is referring to a sunken ship.

In some ways, this is the most delightful of all Nostradamus' attempts to describe something that was scarcely dreamed of in his day. He is picturing a ship (*classe*) which, even when under water (*submergee*), is quite capable of making progress. In modern terms, this is, of course, a submarine.

Note how economical Nostradamus is with his words; he does not tell us that this ship of the future will "sail," but that it will "swim" (*nagera*). The whole point of the old sailing ships is that they were carried by the wind. In contrast, a submarine cannot have sails, and must navigate by some other means.

If we bring together this fourth line with the first, we presume that Nostradamus is predicting an explosion relating to a submarine. Either a submarine will explode, or a submarine will cause an explosion.

By now, it will be evident that Nostradamus had the uncanny ability to foresee key events, and "firsts." Even had it been possible, it would have been tedious for him to write about all the explosions pertaining to submarines in, for example, World War I and World War II. Let us therefore assume that he is writing about the *first* submarine explosion in history.

The first attempted explosion was engineered in 1776, during the American War of Independence. The submarine, designed by David Bushnell, had been brought to New York, from Saybrook, Connecticut. His aim was to sink the English warship *Eagle*, anchored off New York. David's brother, Ezra, had trained long and hard to handle the ungainly submarine. Unfortunately, he fell ill shortly before the planned departure. At this point, a Connecticut general, Samuel Parsons, persuaded his brother-in-law to volunteer. Sergeant Ezra Lee, and two other soldiers, "whom history has failed to name," undertook the dangerous mission.[125] After some rapid, and much-needed training of the new crew, the submarine, appropriately named *Turtle*, was carried by wagon overland from New Rochelle to Kingsbridge, on the Hudson.

On September 6, the *Turtle* was lowered into the water at South Ferry, carrying a barrel of 150 pounds of powder and a timer, designed to control the explosions. When night fell, the *Turtle* was towed into the bay, as near to the British ship as possible, and cast off. In spite of adverse strong tides, Lee managed to reach the hull of the *Eagle*. It was only when he tried to screw the explosive device into the wood of the ship that he realized that it was actually sheathed in copper.[126] He was compelled to jettison the charges, which exploded without doing any damage. Happily, the courageous Lee escaped, and returned back to the American-held lines. However, although this was the "first" explosion caused by a submarine, it was not successful, in the sense that it did not attain its aim of destroying an enemy ship.

Not surprisingly, this event—unsuccessful in itself, yet of such importance to naval history—does not appear to be supported by details given by Nostradamus in the rest of the quatrain. We must presume, therefore, that the prophet had some other submarine in mind.

The first recorded *successful* explosion caused by a submarine took place during the American Civil War, in the dark hours of February 17, 1864. The *Housatonic*, a federal corvette then blockading Charleston, was sunk and destroyed by a torpedo that had been fitted over the spar of a submarine. This was the *Hunley*, designed by the Confederates and driven by a screw manually operated by eight volunteers, with one navigator. Unfortunately, after causing the devastating explosion, the ungainly submarine was swamped, due to a badly fitted hatch, and the nine-man crew perished. An illustration based on a painting of the *Hunley* is now preserved in the Museum of the Confederacy, in Richmond, Virginia.

Now there are certain echoes in the remaining lines of the quatrain that seem to point to this dramatic sinking of the *Housatonic*.

In the first line, after opening with the explosion (*fouldre*), Nostradamus describes an event in the heavens:

Par fouldre en l'arche or, & argent fondu,

By lightning in the arc, gold and silver fused,

This literally means, "in the arc, gold and silver melted (or fused) together." It is an example of Nostradamus setting down astrological data in an obscure way, to befuddle his readers. *L'arche* is the bow (*arc*) of the Archer, otherwise known as Sagittarius.

In the 16th century, Sagittarius was not always represented as a horse-man, or as a bowman, mounted on the back of a horse. In some cases, he was represented in the form of an archer, with goat-like legs. A good example is that depicted behind Nostradamus in the woodcut reproduced on page 8.

This portrait of Nostradamus is from a copy of a work on eclipses, which he published in 1558.[127] It is of value here, for two reasons. First, the illustration pertains to the idea of an eclipse (one is seen near to reaching *defaut*, in the top right-hand corner of the portrait). Secondly, the image of Sagittarius (middle of the left-hand vertical of the zodiacal surround) places emphasis upon *l'arche*, or bow, with which the archer shoots.

The gold (*or*) is the Sun, while the silver (*argent*) is the Moon. This identification of planets with metals is basic lore in the alchemy with which Nostradamus was familiar. The merging, or fusing, of the Sun and Moon (of Gold and Silver) in the alchemical literature is well illustrated in an engraving (see facing page) from a book on the art published in 1622, but using images from earlier sources.[128]

In this arcane figure, the bicorporeal figure represents the unified Sun and Moon. This represents the
human being who has perfected himself by harmoniz-
ing the male (solar) and female (lunar) sides of his nature. Such a man is truly said to have learned how to
control the demon of passions (at his feet).

In strictly astronomical terms, if the Sun and the
Moon are fused together, then they are involved in an
eclipse—either in a solar eclipse, or in a lunar eclipse.
Nostradamus tells us that this *fondu* takes place in the
zodiacal sign Sagittarius. Now, while eclipses are not at
all uncommon, eclipses, when specified in particular
signs, are relatively uncommon. As it happens, in 1864,
there *was* a lunar eclipse in the first degree of Sagittarius. There would be no further lunar eclipse in that
same degree of Sagittarius for well over two centuries.[129]

This astrological data offers us a confirmation that the subject of the quatrain is linked with 1864.

> *De la cité le plus grand estendu,*

> *Of the most grand city extended,*

What is this city, the most extended (*la cité le plus grand estendu,*)? Furthermore, what has this city to do with the *Housatonic*?

The American ship was named after the river, which flows into Long Island Sound, to the northeast of the city of New York. It debouches between Bridgeport and New Haven, Connecticut. From this, we may presume that the city intended by Nostradamus is New York—"the most extended city," at the tip of a long and extended island. This is not only because it is, so to speak, off Long Island—a geographical feature very well described as *estendu*. It is also because it is far distant from its namesake York, in England, and (presumably) because it was far distant from France, where Nostradamus was writing.

> *Des deux captifz l'un l'autre mangera,*

> *The two captives will devour one another,*

What about the cannibalism implicit in the second line? Who are the two captives (*deux captifz*) who will eat one another (*l'un l'autre mangera*)?

This second line can be read as an extension of the first, which means that there really is no cannibalism. It is the Sun (*or*) and the Moon (*argent*) who will seem to devour each other, in the eclipse. It is, of course, an old idea—old even when Nostradamus wrote—that the Sun was swallowed up by the Moon during a solar eclipse, or that the Moon was devoured by the Earth during a lunar eclipse.[130] What is important in this line is not the idea of cannibalism, but of those cannibalized being captives (*captifz*).

They are described as captives because the phenomenon of the eclipse has just been "captured," in the very first degree of Sagittarius. But what if the curious spelling of *captifz*, which appears only in the early editions published in Nostradamus' own lifetime, has something to do with the technical astrological word *syzygy*, which, in the 16th century, meant "coming together in the same degree of the Sun and Moon"?[131] The original Greek, συζυγια (syzygia), meant "yoke," or "being tied together"—thus, captive.

The idea of this type of "capture" is reflected in Nostradamus' emphasis of the hunting weapon held by Sagittarius—l'arche, or bow. He is the hunter, who makes captives of the things he hunts.

One can't help but wonder if Nostradamus is playing, almost wickedly, with the name of the condemned ship. There is no word similar to *Housatonic* in French. However, bearing in mind that the French do not pronounce the initial aspirate, the sound might be read, in the secret language of encoding that Nostradamus used, as a combination, or portmanteau, word.[132]

By combining *ousseau* (cut to *oussa* by the rule of aphesis) with *tonic* (a version of *tonique*), we obtain the construct *oussatonic*. The first part of this construct, *ousseau*, is a naval term, meaning the "well of a ship." *Tonique*, like the English tonic, means "keynote." Without too much distortion of meaning, we may see that the keynote of this quatrain deals with the consequences of there being an explosion (*fouldre*) in the well of a ship.

Man's First Flight

•

Nostradamus's interest in modern inventions extended well beyond such things as submarines. He was deeply interested in the idea of flight—indeed, in what in his day was the seeming impossibility of heavier-than-air flight. He touches on the invention of airplanes in a number of quatrains, but nowhere so gracefully as in quatrain III.5.

> *Pres loin default de deux grās luminaires*
> *Qui surviendra entre Avril & Mars:*
> *O quel cherté mais deux grās debōnaires*
> *Par terre & mer secourront toutes pars.*[133]

For the moment, we'll translate this as:

> *Not far from the deficiency of the two great lumi-*
> *naires*
> *Which will occur between April and March,*
> *O, at what cost, but two great debonaires*
> *By earth and sea will secure all parts.*

A casual reading will suggest that Nostradamus is dating the events predicted within the quatrain by means of a solar eclipse (a *default* or "weakening" of sunlight, when the Moon passes in front of the Sun).[134] This kind of dating is not very helpful, however. As we have seen, eclipses occur very frequently. There can be as many as five solar eclipses in a single year.

The first line gives the timing, but it is not a time frame with which the modern reader is usually familiar. Once again, Nostradamus is using the dating system put into print in 1522 by the arcanist Trithemius. It is a system he uses quite often in his quatrains, and one we have already examined, in relation to the Nostradamus quatrains (see pages 70 and 94).

According to this system, the Moon will reach the end of its cycle in either 1880 or 1881, and the Sun will take over. Nostradamus seems to be visualizing this meeting together of Moon and Sun (the past and the future) as a sort of eclipse, a weakening in light (a *default*).[135]

In terms of the planetary rulers named by Trithemius, this means that Gabriel will hand over his rule to Michael.

As we have seen, the Trithemian period is 354 years and 4 months. According to Trithemius, the lunar period began in 1525 and 4 months. This latter seems to have been a miscalculation, and the period should have been 1525. Nostradamus seems to have been aware of this discrepancy, and proposed that the change from Moon to Sun would take place in 1880 and four months—that is, April 1880. According to his verse, the change over, the *default*, or eclipse of Sun and Moon, would happen between March and April (*surviendra entre Avril & Mars*). This explains the reference to April, the "fourth month," in the modern calendar.[136]

Is there any event, occurring in or near (*pres loing*) 1880 that makes sense, within the framework of the rest of the verse?

Pres loin default de deux grās luminaires

Not far from the deficiency of the two great luminaires

The *luminaires* are the "luminaries," a word used frequently in medieval astrology for the Sun and Moon. The *default* is a sort of eclipse, when the two come together, and cancel each other out for a short while. Nostradamus probably did not use the traditional French word, *eclipse*, to denote the event he had in mind, simply because he was interested in another phenomenon involving the coming together of the luminaries.

According to the Trithemian cycles, there is only one transfer of rulership from Moon to Sun in 2,480 years! This occurred in about 1880, or 1881.

deux grās debōnaires

Two grand debonnaires

With the word *grands*, Nostradamus had in mind great men (*grandes* would be great women)—aristocrats, or remarkable people. The word *debonnaires*, which at first seems so puzzling, is actually a most useful clue to the theme of the quatrain. In the 16th century, it still carried the original connotation of *de bonne aire* (of a good air), of a good mien. However, in the 16th century, the word air also meant "air," in the sense of the familiar gaseous mixture we breathe. We may conclude from this that the "remarkable people of good air" to which Nostradamus refers are those who pioneered flight, toward the end of the 19th century.

That Nostradamus is inviting this reading is evident from the care he has taken to make *aire* a feminine noun. This he has done by insisting on the form *debōnaires*, which has the effect of doubling the n, to read *debonnaires* (*de bonne aires*). Had he not been interested in drawing our attention to the word, he need never have included the grammatically incorrect abbreviation mark.

The history of heavier-than-air flight is, of course, a complex one, for the first successful flight of such a machine was preceded by the invention of several working models. The extraordinary thing, from a point of view of the Nostradamus prophecy, is that heavier-than-air flight was successfully achieved at the point where the lunar period ended, and the solar period began.

Nostradamus had written that the event in quatrain III.5 would be close to (*pres loin*) the period he described. Shortly before 1880, Victor Tatin flew an airplane with a wingspan of just over 6 feet for a distance of about 100 feet, somewhat similar to the one he used in his manual on aviation (see facing page).

Even while Tatin was experimenting, the multigifted Samuel Pierpont Langley, the astronomer and physicist, was experimenting with flight, at the Allegheny observatory in Pennsylvania. In 1896, while secretary of the Smithsonian, in Washington, D.C., he constructed a machine, driven by steam, which flew for

ELÉMENTS

D'AVIATION

PAR

VICTOR TATIN

about half a mile along the Potomac River. This plane was unmanned, but what was learned from it helped the Wright brothers, of Dayton, Ohio, achieve their own epoch-making breakthrough.

By means of his three words *deux grands debonnaires*, Nostradamus is referring to *two* great ones (men of good air). Were it not for the specific date, close to 1880, we might be inclined to think that he was writing a quatrain about the Wright brothers. However, given the specific time frame, my suspicion is that he was writing of Tatin and Hargrave, both of whom flew heavier-than air machines driven by compressed air, similar to the one reproduced on page 136, from Tatin's book.

These flights not only emphasize in a new way the concept of air (*de bonne aires*), but were also undertaken on either side of the key date. Tatin flew his model for about 100 feet, in 1879. Hargrave flew his

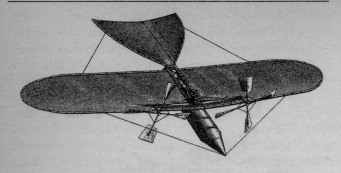

No. 16 for 343 feet, in 1885. Given that the Secundadeian time sequence of rulerships is not repeated for over 2,480 years, the precision of Nostradamus's dating is uncanny in its accuracy.

The precision of Nostradamus's final line has now become clear. In the 16th century, it was virtually impossible to journey in a single mechanical device by both land and sea (*terre & mer*). After 1880 such a single mode of travel had became possible, and would shortly become an actual reality. By means of air flight, it was possible to "secour all directions, or parts of the world" (*secourront toutes pars*). In this three-word phrase, Nostradamus yet again reveals his genius. The verb *secourrir* certainly means "to secour," but originally, it meant to "speed oneself," figuratively, "to fly."[137] How else might one run over earth and sea, in such a way, were it not by means of air?

The expression *O quel cherté*, in the third line of the quatrain, may appear to be especially peculiar, in this context of flight. However, it is yet another sign of the genius with which Nostradamus worked. Before examining the phrase, it should be noted that several early printings of this quatrain offer variants of this phrase. Among these is the variant, which appeared as early as 1558, *cherré*.[138] It would not be a surprise if this were the word Nostradamus had actually used when penning the verse. Remarkably, the French verb *cherrer*, which in the 16th century meant "to exaggerate," has been adopted to a reading that makes sense of the quatrain, written four centuries earlier. In the post-1880 phase of civilization, *cherrer* came into use as a specialized term in aviation. It now means "to do stunts," or acrobatics in the air!

The Space Program

•

Verse X.74 is utterly fascinating, if only because a superficial reading might suggest an apocalyptic end for mankind. In view of this, it is perhaps understandable (if regrettable), that Roberts should see the quatrain as predicting that the dead will rise up, in 2007 AD. Unfortunately, he gives no indication as to how he arrived at this now-imminent year. In fact, the verse deals with a substantial, and beneficial, scientific achievement.

An revolu du grand nombre septiesme,
Apparoistra au temps jeux d'Hecatombe,
Non esloigne du grand aage milliesme,
Que les entrez sortiront de leur tombe.[139]

The revolution year of the great number seventh,
Will appear at the time of the game of the
Hecatombe,
Not far from the great millennium age,
That [those] who enter will come out of their
tomb.

The year in question truly was a year of revolution (*an revolu*) in more senses than one. The first line seems to refer to a date for the event to be predicted, for it mentions a year (*An*). It is a year in which there is a "revolution" of the great seventh number (*grand nombre septiesme*). We shall see, eventually, that the word *revolu* has at least two meanings. The most important of these, which permits us to offer a date for the quatrain, is again a reference to the dating system of Trithemius.

Nostradamus, while referring in a guarded manner to the system of planetary angels proposed by Trithemius, had used the word *revolution* more than once.[140] These, as he makes clear, are "calculations of times," and occasionally, "astronomical calculations." Within this context, the word revolution can have two meanings. It can relate to the series of great ages governed by the seven planetary angels (a periodicity of 7×354 years). It can also refer to the individual rulership, or "revolution," of 354 years that is marked by each of these cycles. As we shall see, each of these two diffcrent forms of revolution are mentioned in this quatrain, and for this reason I shall examine both here.

Trithemius, following medieval belief, accepted that the world was created on March 15, 5560 BC. Since that time, the seven angels had ruled epochs of 354 years and 4 months, in sequence, starting with Saturn, and ending with Sun. In all, between 5560 BC and 2235 AD, each angel will have ruled, in their own sequence, three times. This is why Nostradamus can refer to the "grand number" (*grand nombre*) in the first line. This grand number is 21, which in numerology reduces to the magical 3 ($2 + 1 = 3$), and which is itself a product of $3 \times 7 = 21$.

The revolution is also used to determine the individual rule, or cycle, of any given angel. We are living under the rulership of Michael, the angel of the Sun. This Michaelic rulership commenced its third *revolution* in 1880. In other words, mankind presently lives in the period marked by the revolution of the "seventh period of the great number" (*grand nombre septiesme*).

	ANGEL	PLANET	DATE OF RULERSHIP
1	Ophiel	Saturn	600 BC to 245 BC

[Birth of Christ during rulership of Saturn]

2	Anael	Venus	109 AD to 463 AD
3	Zachariel	Jupiter	463 AD to 817 AD
4	Raphael	Mercury	817 AD to 1172 AD
5	Samael	Mars	1171 AD to 1525 AD
6	Gabriel	Moon	1525 AD to 1880 AD
7	Michael	Sun	1880 AD to 2235 AD
8	Ophiel	Saturn	2235 AD to 2589 AD
9	Anael	Venus	2589 AD to 2944 AD

In sum, the *seventh* great number is that of the solar angel Michael, who began his rule in 1880. According to the time system used by Trithemius, this was the 7086 year after the creation of the world. The first line of the quatrain is therefore intended to be misleading. It opens by suggesting a reference to a year (*An*), but in fact it reveals only a period. The predicted event is to fall sometime in the period after this year 1880, and before its end, in 2235. Perhaps we should translate the first line of the quatrain to accommodate this, as follows:

A year in the revolution of the great number seventh,

Nostradamus himself, by referring to a year (*An*), is clearly specifying a particular year in that solar revolution of 354 years under the rule of Michael. It is evident that such a vast period needs some qualification, if we are to successfully date the prediction within the verse. Later, we shall study one good reason why Nostradamus approached the dating in this cumbersome-seeming way.

The third line of the verse seems to qualify this period. According to Nostradamus, the predicted event is to take place "not far from the great age of the millennium." Once again, the notion of the great age is involved with the numerology of the magical seven. The "great age" occurs in the seventh millennium. In terms of the Christian calendar, the seventh millennium fell in 2000 (properly speaking, in terms of calendrical measurements, it fell in 2001). We may take it, therefore, that Nostradamus is writing about a future event that will take place "not far from" the year 2000 or 2001.

While Nostradamus has given us only a general idea of the year he has in mind, he is very specific about the time of year (that is, the month) when this predicted event will take place.

He tells us that:

Apparoistra au temps jeux d'Hecatombe,

There will appear at the time of the game of the Hecatomb . . .

Etymologically, the word *hecatomb* refers to the slaughter of a hundred cattle. In ancient times, such a mass bloodletting was a prelude to certain important festivities, or offered by priests in recognition of a need to sacrifice to the gods.[141] In modern times, the word has been applied to the slaughter of men, as well as animals: modern warfare is sometimes described as hecatombs.[142]

It is very likely that Nostradamus was using the word in its original, and very specific, sense, in order to specify a date for the predicted event. In ancient Greece, the opening of the Olympic year saw such a sacrifice of a hundred oxen. This gruesome ritual was called the *hecatombeon*. It is one of the few ancient hecatombs to be associated with a specific date. The date of the Olympics was determined by a lunar calendar, and so the event itself was movable, within certain fixed limits. There is much dispute among scholars as to the dates on which the Olympics were staged. It has been proposed that these dates were determined by the time of the first full moon following the summer solstice, and was generally dated in terms of the Elean calendar.[143] Given the context of the quatrain, there is no doubt that Nostradamus had in mind the full moon in the Elean calendar, which fell in the month of *Apollonios*, sacred to the sun god Apollo. This full moon fell between August 6 and September 5, in the modern calendrical system.

The second century AD Greek traveler, Pausanias, who wrote fairly extensively on the Olympic Games, was surprisingly vague as to how the event was fixed in time. In spite of this, given that Nostradamus was attempting to suggest a date that would be clear to any of his contemporaries who sought to unravel the meaning of the verse, we must presume that this date must relate to what Pausanias wrote. The alternative, of linking the date with modern scholarly speculation, en-

riched by discoveries made at Olympia in the archaeo-
logical digs of the late 19th century, seems chimerical.

The general view, based on what Pausanias wrote, is
that the *hecatombeon* corresponded to the last part of
July and the beginning of August, in the modern calendar.[144] The main sacrifices themselves took place on the
first and fifth days of the Olympics.[145]

Although Nostradamus has spent three lines setting
out this date, it seems that he is referring to a time in
July or August, not far from (*Non esloigne du*) 2000 or
2001. The predicted date seems to hinge on what Nostradamus meant by the vaguely expressed "not far
from." Is it possible that we can tell, from the fourth
line, what this future event might be, in order to nar-
row the time of the event?

At first glance, the fourth line does seem to be apocalyptic. It reminds one of the high drama of the Bible,
in which such authors as St. John and St. Matthew
wrote of the moment of resurrection, when the dead
"that are in the graves," shall come forth.[146]

The key words in this fourth line seem to be *entrez*
and *tombe*. Let us examine them both. Because of the
peculiar way in which Nostradamus usually writes, *entrez* could mean "we enter," or simply "entrance." It can
also mean to pass from one state into another.

Is there any specialized use of the word *entrez*, which
will throw light on the fourth line of the quatrain?
There are two rather specialist uses of the word, both of
which appear to be relevant to the verse.

In Pausanias's description of the ancient city of

Corinth, on Peloponnisos—a city one is likely to pass through on a land journey to Olympia—he describes a gateway to the city. On top of the arch of the gate is represented a pair of four-horsed chariots. One depicted Phaethon, the son of the Sun god, and the other Apollo himself. As a matter of fact, this Corinthian doorway is represented on copper coinage of several Roman emperors.[147]

As it is evident from other references that Nostradamus was familiar with Pausanias's descriptions of Greece, we may take it that the doorway by which one may enter and leave (*entrez sortiront*) is this Corinthian portal, dominated by solar image. In his Greek text, Pausanias mentions the solar god by his Greek name, Helios, but any 16th-century scholar would recognize this as the Apollo of the Romans.

Nostradamus seems to be drawing our attention to the god Apollo, who dominates the entrance to the city of Corinth, with his chariot of the Sun. It is perhaps this reference, which incorporates not merely a reference to the Sun god, but also to his unfortunate son, Phaethon, which may explain the reference to "tomb" in this final line. As we have already seen, in connection with another quatrain, on page 38, Phaethon met his death in consequence of his overweening ambition— daring to drive the chariot that only his father could handle. In the event predicted, however, there will be no such death, for those who make this daring trip, leaving by and returning to, the chariots of the Sun, will survive—*they will come out of the tomb.*

Que les entrez sortiront de leur tombe.[148]

That [those] who enter will come out of their tomb.

This reference to the gate of the Sun god at Corinth explains the context of the Nostradamian line very well. However, Nostradamus seems to have evoked a different literary source to reflect on the idea of entering and returning.

One does not "enter" a tomb willingly: usually, interment is a very passive thing. In the esoteric literature with which Nostradamus was familiar, it was claimed that one entered into life, and made an exit from life at the point of death. In a short, but influential essay by Porphyry, called *De Antro*, it was said that at birth, one entered into the world by the door of Cancer, and at death, one left the world by the door of Saturn.

> *Theologists therefore assert that these two gates are Cancer and Capricorn; but Plato calls them entrances. And of these theologists say that Cancer is the gate through which souls descend, but Capricorn is that through which they ascend.*[149]

Now, Nostradamus is writing about individuals who did *not* die. These people came out of their tomb (*sortiront de leur tombe*).[150] In view of this, we must presume that he has in mind the door of Cancer. Cancer is ruled by the Moon, and in some literature the "birth gate" is actually called the Portal of the Moon. This suggests that the quatrain must have some thing to do with the Moon. It suggests, further, that the emphasis in the first three lines on the solar archangel, Michael, invites some connection with the Sun, or with the Roman pagan deity Apollo.

In view of this, we must look for an event, during the period stipulated, which is connected with both the Moon and Apollo.

* * *

All these conditions are surely applicable to those astronauts who flew on the Apollo missions, in the 1960s, for in this both the Sun and the Moon came together. Apollo was the pagan Roman name for the Sun God. These astronauts quite literally entered space by way of the Moon, and returned to Earth.

Such a reading makes sense of the word *tombe*, for the spacecraft resembles a tomb, in which the individual within is sealed off from the world.[151] The craft also seems to "fall" (*tomber*) in space, first toward the Moon and then back, toward the Earth. Indeed, the technical term for the falling descent of craft, through the atmosphere of the earth is, in both French and English "entry" (*entrez*—properly speaking, *entrée*)—a word that appears in the final line.

On the assumption that Nostradamus had in mind such a lunar space probe, let us examine the quatrain once more, to see what we may learn from its structure and dating.

An revolu now takes on a new meaning. We are dealing not only with the revolution of the ages, but also with the revolution of a spacecraft. Not only is it possible to describe the outward and inward voyage to the Moon as a revolution, but in some instances, the craft would make revolutions, or circuits, of the Moon. For example, while Neil Armstrong and Edwin "Buzz" Aldrin Jr. walked upon the surface of the Moon, in 1969, Michael Collins kept the mother craft in circuit around the Moon.

Before examining in more detail this exciting possibility that Nostradamus was predicting space flight, let us recapitulate on the timing within the quatrain.

In terms of the vast Trithemian cycles (*revolutions*) of the planetary angels, the period between 1880 and 2235 marks the seventh period (*nombre septiesme*).

In terms of the years, the seventh (*nombre septiesme*) in the 20th century is that decade beginning with 1970. This decade is itself not far removed from the millennium of 2001, as specified in the third line of the quatrain. The years 1968 to 1971 fall within this period.

If we examine the lunar probes made during the Apollo program, we find that it was that conducted by Apollo 11, in July 16–24, 1969, which brought the program to its successful culmination. On July 20 of that year, Neil Armstrong was the first human being to step on to the surface of the Moon.

July is the seventh month (*nombre septiesme*), and it is also the month linked, in ancient times, with the date of the Hecatomb. In effect, this date makes convincing sense of the first three lines of the quatrain.

While there should be no doubt that Nostradamus has referred to the *hecatomb* in order to offer a firm dating for his predicted event, the word contains another meaning. The fact is that the word is linked in the Greek language with the Sun god Apollo. One Greek epithet used for Apollo was *ekatombaios*, "one to whom hecatombs were offered." Another such epithet for Apollo was εκαιος (hecatos), and is said to be a shortened form of the Greek meaning "far-darting"—an excellent phrase in regard to the distant journeys of the Apollo probes.

*   *   *

We are now in a better position to see why Nostradamus did not specify a particular date, but, as it were, a window in time. The Apollo 11 lunar landing of July 1969 was one of a series in an extensive program. This reference to space flight helps us understand the other curious word in the last line of the quatrain—*tombe*.

The word *tombe*, which we translate here as *tomb*, could equally well read *tombeau*, in French. In the French versions of St. John's and Matthew's gospels, the equivalent word is given as *sepulchre*. Even given that Nostradamus was prepared to change French words to suit his purpose, we should ask why he uses this phrase in the singular. Possibly because the word *tombe* has a second meaning, which the word *tombeau* does not have. The French *tombe* (from the verb *tomber*), also means "fall." Nostradamus often omits the accents from words that have them in our modern orthography. In view of this, we may assume that the word we translate as "grave" may also mean "fall."

Unlike St. John, Nostradamus refers to the *tombe* in the singular, as though there were only one tomb: it is extremely likely that he was using the singular merely in order to rhyme with the Hecatomb of the second line.[152] Furthermore, St. John had not written about these resurrected "entering" the tombs. The line cannot be construed as merely a reference to the Biblical text, for it contains several variants, and suggests too many queries. Perhaps, given the context of space flight, we should be tempted to read the French *tombe* not primarily as a reference to an entombment, or burial, but to a "fall"—that is, a fall through space. If we do this, we are offered the intriguing prospect that Nostradamus was predicting the successful Apollo space program, wherein the space capsules "fell" to earth safely.

The name of the series, Apollo, is highly relevant to the quatrain. Nostradamus is writing about the revolution of the *grand nombre septiesme*, which is actually marked by the archangel of the Sun. This is one reason why of all the numerous lunar missions, it is the Apollo series to which Nostradamus refers. Apollo seems to be the perfect choice, even in the face of the earlier Gemini series of launches (none of which landed on the Moon), and the Russian series. Of these, Soyuz 1 does not fulfil the requirements set out by Nostradamus, for at re-entry (April 24, 1967) the parachutes fouled, the spacecraft crashed, and Vladimir M. Komarov was killed.

It is intriguing, in view of the numerology adopted by Nostradamus, that the first crewed flight under the Apollo command was undertaken in Apollo 7, in 1968. This is one relevant *septiesme*. A later Apollo attempt ended in failure, yet still enabled those inside the capsule to return to earth. This was Apollo 13, the seventh in the series. On April 11, 1970, Apollo 13 blasted off on the third crewed trip to the Moon; well into the flight, a rupture of a fuel-cell oxygen tank forced the astronauts to abort the trip. They succeeded in returning to the Earth in the lunar module life-support system.

Of the eleven Apollo manned trips on record, only two took place during the July-August window specified by the quatrain. The sequence below makes this clear:

Apollo 7	Oct. 11–Oct. 22, 1968
Apollo 8	Dec. 21–Dec. 27, 1968
Apollo 9	Feb. 28–Mar. 13, 1969
Apollo 10	May 18–May 26, 1969
Apollo 11	Jul. 16–Jul. 24, 1969
Apollo 12	Nov. 14–Nov. 22, 1969
Apollo 13	Apr. 11–Apr. 17, 1970
Apollo 14	Jan. 31–Feb. 9, 1971
Apollo 15	Jul. 26–Aug. 7, 1971[153]
Apollo 16	Apr. 16–Apr. 27, 1972
Apollo 17	Dec. 7–Dec. 19, 1972

We see that of all these flights in the Apollo program, only two correspond, in terms of dating, with the limitations set down by Nostradamus, in relation to the *Hecatomb* dating we have examined. These are Apollo 11 and Apollo 15. It seems that Nostradamus was interested mainly in the successful Moon landing of Apollo 11. This impression is rooted in the fact that the various themes set out in the quatrain—the theme of Apollo, of the Moon, of the entrance and return, and the all-important dates of July/August—are fulfilled in the Apollo 11 project.

Now, the fascinating thing about all these 11 Apollo programs is that, in spite of the incredible difficulties involved in these lunar missions, not a single astronaut lost his life. In every case, they were (to paraphrase Nostradamus) able to make their *entry*, and *come out of their fall*.

In fact, in terms of the dating contained within the quatrain, there are only two possible flights we might consider as being relevant to the verse. Both flights were successful, in terms of mission aims, but it is evident that the prize must be given to Apollo 11 as the first to land humans on the Moon.

There is one necessary word of caution about the interpretation of this verse. For once, Nostradamus was not precise about the year for the prophecy. He was fairly precise about the time of year, and about the period in which the event[s] would occur, but he allowed a certain latitude. Perhaps he allowed this latitude because the Apollo program was spread over a number of years, from 1968 to 1972. However, this very latitude permits an element of doubt. It remains a possibility that he was referring to some event[s] *after* the millennium of 2000.

The entry into the Earth's atmosphere of Russia's aging space station, *Mir*, which crashed into the Pacific in March 2001, partly fits the requirements of the quatrain. The *Mir* had a working lifetime of about 15 years, and over a hundred astronauts spent time in her.[154] The entry and burning up of the *Mir* was planned and controlled by the Russian Aerospace Agency; since all astronauts had left the ship long before she was scuttled in this way, the last line of the quatrain does not seem to be as valid as for the Apollo projects. Only time will tell if there is some other undertaking—presumably involving the exploration of space—which will make even more sense of this quatrain.

Conclusion

•

At the very beginning of this book, I mentioned the dragon-star Rastaban, so deeply involved in the terrible events that occurred in New York, on September 11, 2001. I intimated, then, that I would return to the subject of astrology. I have no inclination to write about the horoscope of this terrible event at the moment. I am sure that many astrologers will take it upon themselves to write and talk openly about this, and the related charts. Rather than discuss the horoscope, I would like to write a few words about fixed stars that were operative at the time. I do this mainly out of respect for Nostradamus, but also because of the astonishing symbolism that pervaded this act of terrorism, in a cosmic sense.

Nostradamus not only referred to the fixed stars in his quatrains, but, on occasion, also named them. Usually, he did this for some symbolic purposes.[155] Like most 16th-century astrologers, he used the stars in the many personal horoscopes he cast for his clients.[156]

This was expected of him. The astrology of the 16th century placed much more emphasis on stellar lore than do modern astrologers. The astrologers of that time recognized that, without a careful consideration of the influence of fixed stars, the reading of personal horoscopes is usually rendered almost vacuous.

At the time of the destruction of two towers in Manhattan by terrorists, the evil star Rastaban was conjunct with the dark planet Pluto. There were other stellar influences at work at that time, and all these should be studied by those interested in astrology. However, there was one really astonishing stellar influence, which should not go unnoticed even by those not interested in astrology. At 8:45 A.M., on Tuesday, September 11, 2001, the fixed star Sirius was directly overhead.[157]

Sirius, the prime star of Canis Majoris, is far from being an evil star. Indeed, in terms of world history, it is one of the most remarkable stars in the heavens. It was the *Sihor* of the ancient Egyptian civilization, and it was the star that was represented in Rosicrucian and Masonic symbolism as the "blazing star." Even its original sound, in Greek, was representative of this inner flame, for it was the *Seirios* star—the one that sparkled and scorched. Indeed, it is no accident that so many ancient Egyptian temples were oriented to this powerful star. In Nordic mythology, it was the star at which those lovers who built the bridge of the Milky Way from different sides met and were united.[158]

Even today, this Sirius is the most famous star in America. It is the original star behind the symbolism of the familiar five-pointed star, which graces the American flag, the Great Seal of America, and the American dollar bill.

It is not surprising that this primal five-pointed star of blazing Sirius should have been immediately overhead, in the heavens, when the terrorists struck. It was a symbol-star, a thing of brightness where only love could triumph, and where hatred had no place. It was held high in the heavens, announcing that the kind of warped darkness that these men carried in their own souls would never overcome the light. When these men murdered and maimed, for their own private purposes (as no man may murder or maim in the name of a true religion), they did these things oblivious to the fact that the stars look down, and that God sees all.

The promise of the five-pointed star is obvious. It reminds us that, even if wrongdoers are not brought to justice by men, another, far more powerful justice awaits them in the spiritual world. What criminals do not realize is that all crime is nothing more than a temporary expedient, and in the end, love alone conquers all.

Note on Sources

•

I should record the source from which I have taken the quatrains, and the French verses I have recorded in this book. I need to do this because, during the past four centuries, many of the original quatrains have been emended. In some cases, these emendations were due to slipshod editing and poor scholarship. At other times, they were intentionally slipped in by editors, anxious to prove a point, at the expense of Nostradamus. The result is that the vast majority of easily available texts attributed to Nostradamus are quite unreliable.

Wherever possible, I have tried to use the French version of the quatrains that Nostradamus would almost certainly have approved, personally. It is very unlikely that those printers who worked in Lyons (not far from the town of Salon, where Nostradamus lived), would have been printing works without his approval. With this in mind, I have selected the verses from those available in the 1557 edition, printed at Lyons by Antoine du Rosne. This rare work has had a curious history. It has been argued by some modern scholars that this edition was stolen from the State Library in Munich by Adolf Hitler. No doubt this theft took place because Hitler had been alerted to the notion that his own name appeared in a quatrain.[1]

This work of 1557 was not the first edition.[2] Indeed, the most authoritative bibliography of Nostradamus' works lists it as the fifth edition of the *Prophéties*.[3] However, its value to us lies in the fact that, unlike the earlier editions, it contains *seven* of the centuries, rather than merely *three and a half*. This edition is therefore an essential adjunct to the study of the quatrains.[4]

The rare first edition, printed by Macé Bonhomme in 1555, contained less than a third of the quatrains now known to us. It comprised only three complete centuries of verses, along with 53 as part of a fourth century. This work is extremely rare. Until quite recently, it was thought that no examples of the first edition had survived in Europe or the United States. The one that had been used as a basis for scholarship, preserved in the City Library of Paris, was destroyed in a fire, during 1871. The other was stolen from the Mazarin Library in Paris.

Fortunately, in 1984, a first edition (1555) of the *Prophéties* was discovered in the Municipal Library at Albi. An identical example has since been found, conserved in the State Library in Vienna.[5] The texts of both include important differences in the quatrains known to us at the present time, from later editions. In some cases, I have used quatrains derived from the first editions to include the final three centuries, in the canon of ten. These were both published at Lyon, in two separate editions (the sixth and eighth editions, respectively) by Benoît Rigaud and Jean de Tournes.

Notes to Note on Sources

[1] For an account of Hitler and Nostradamus, see Ellic Howe, *Nostradamus and the Nazis. A Footnote to the History of The Third Reich,* 1965.

[2] The scholar Count Carl von Klinckowstroem certainly studied this edition, when it was in the Bayerische Staatsbibliothek München, and it is known that it disappeared during World War II. See Klinckowstroem, "Die ältesten Ausgaben der 'Propheties' des Nostradamus," in *Der Zeitschift für Bücherfreunde,* March 1913. The scholar Daniel Ruzo believes that it was among the many boxes of valuable books once kept at Berchtesgaden, where Hitler lived. See Ruzo, *Le testament de Nostradamus,* 1982. If this were the case, then it is possible that this lost edition is now somewhere in Moscow.

[3] This is the work by Robert Benazra, *Répertoire Chronologique Nostradamique (1545–1989),* 1990.

[4] The modern scholar Michel Chomarat has published a facsimile of this work, *Les Prophéties. Lyons, 1557,* 1993.

[5] The discovery was made by Jacques Pons, conservator of the Muncipal Library in Albi, in response to a general appeal mounted by L'Association Lyonnaise, "Les Amis de Nostradamus." See *Cahiers Michel Nostradamus,* No. 3, Feb., 1985, p. 33.

Bibliographic Notes

●

[1] In 2001, Draconis is located in 11.57 degrees of Sagittarius. On September 11, 2001, Pluto was in 12.38 degrees of Sagittarius.

[2] The tower collapsed at 10:28 A.M.

[3] The supposed verse is not in quatrain form, and is partly a pastiche, built up from poor translations of fragments, abstracted from a number of poor translations, into English, of verses that Nostradamus *did* write. As I received it, the quatrain read:

> *In the year of the new century and nine months, From the sky will come a great King of Terror . . . The sky will burn at forty-five degrees. Fire approaches the great new city. In the city of York there will be a great collapse, 2 twin brothers torn apart by chaos while the fortress falls the great leader will succumb third big war will begin when the big city is burning.*

[4] See Richard Woods, "When death came out of a blue sky," in *The Sunday Times*, September 16, 2001, pp 4ff—the forged quatrains are given on p. 7. Woods was quite wrong in claiming that the two quatrains he recorded "correspond roughly to a verse in Nostradamus." The first one he published is nothing more than a bowdlerized version of a line from quatrain VI.97, which I deal with myself: however, the original French does not mention "the year of the new century and nine months," and not one of the four lines is translated accurately. Both are pastiches, and correspond fairly closely to the non-Nostradamian text that was faxed to me

from the United States. Nostradamus never mentioned "a third big war." The second verse he records is nothing more than a pastiche, in what I can only describe as the pseudo-manner of Nostradamus. At the expense of ironically being taxed for breaching someone's copyright, I reproduce these verses, below:

> *In the year of the new century and nine months*
> *From the sky will come a great King of Terror*
> *The sky will burn at forty-five degrees*
> *Fire approaches the new city.*

> *In the City of God there will be a great thunder*
> *Two brothers torn apart by chaos*
> *While the fortress endures, the great leader will succumb*
> *The third big war will begin when the big city is burning.*

[5] This is Roberts' treatment of quatrain I.87. See Henry C. Roberts, *The Complete Prophecies of Nostradamus*, in the 1982 edn. Roberts had not used an early Nostradamus text for his French versions of the verses, nor had he translated these (as he pretended he had). Both the French and the English have been badly adapted from the 1671 edition of Theophiliius Garencières, *The True Prophecies or Prognostications of Michael Nostradamus*, 1672. This was the first translation of all the *Prophéties* into English. Unfortunately, this work is extremely poor in both its English rendition of the verses, and in the transmission of the French, which frequently differs widely from what Nostradamus wrote.

[6] This was Roberts' commentary on quatrain II.54—see p. 83.

[7] This was Roberts' commentary on quatrain II.91—see p. 92.

[8] The first edition of *Les Propheties de M. Michel Nostradamus* was published by Macé Bonhomme at Lyons, in 1555. This contained the first three centuries, along with a fourth incomplete century, of 53 quatrains. The fifth edition of this first work, published by Antoine du Rosne, in 1557, contained the first five centuries, a sixth with only 99 quatrains, and a seventh with only 40 quatrains. It was the sixth edition, published at Lyon, in 1558, which first set out the 10 quatrains, but these were not all complete. After the death of Nostradamus, in 1566, other quatrains (sometimes of questionable origin and dubious authorship) were added to subsequent editions. The literature on the subject is both vast and complex. The major

work of scholarship on the Nostradamus oeuvre, which lists books up to 1989, consists of 634 closely printed pages: see Robert Benazra, *Répertoire Chronologique Nostradamique (1545–1989)*, 1990.

[9] The portrait, attributed to Leonard Gaultier, is number 129 from a series of 144 portraits of famous men, published in Claude de Valle, *Le Théâtre d'Honneur du plusieurs princes anciens at modernes . . .* 1618.

[10] There is no satisfactory or reliable life of Nostradamus. Most of the claims made about his life in potted biographies are at best unsupported by documentation, at worst fantasist. For an account of some reliably documented material, see Edgar Leroy, *Nostradamus. Ses origins. Sa vie. Son oeuvre*, 1993 impression of 1972 edn.

[11] I have taken this from the 1557 edition of *Les Propheties de M. Michel Nostradamus*, printed by Antoine du Rosne, 1557. By the edition of 1558 there had been a few editorial adjustments—mainly, the removal of abbreviations, and the capitalization of *Normans*. I reproduce below a sample of the 1558 version, which was the one that was transmitted, with only slight variations, over the following centuries.

> *Cinq & quarante degrez ciel bruslera,*
> *Feu approcher de la grand' cité neuve,*
> *Instant grand flamme esparse sautera,*
> *Quand on voudra des Normans faire preuve.*

[12] The text is available only in the 1602 edition of John Brereton, *A brief and true relation;* see, however, David Beers Quinn (ed), *The Roanoke Voyages 1584–1590*, 1955, p. 461. The Raleigh arms is on *La Virgenia Pars*.

[13] For the Dee map, see Quinn, op. cit., n. 12 above, p. 461.

[14] I give a list of the Gauricus latitudes in my work, *The Secrets of Nostradamus*, 2001, p. 401.

[15] Montreal is 45 degrees and 30 seconds north.

[16] Grenoble is on 45 degrees, ten minutes; Marseille is on 43 degrees, 18 minutes.

[17] This map is *Orbis Terrarum ad mentem Ptolemaei*, based on coordinates available in the 15th century, but formulated in the second century.

[18] This is Jacopo le Moyne de Mogues' map, *Floridae Americae Provincae* (from his *Brevis narratio*), which is reproduced by Stefan

Lorant (ed.) in *The New World. The First Pictures of America. Made by John White and Jacques le Moyne and Engraved by Theodore de Bry*, 1946, pp. 34–5.

[19] The Capitol Building is on 38 degrees, 53 minutes, 24 seconds, north.

[20] Boston lies on 42 degrees, 21 minutes, 30 seconds, north.

[21] New York is on 40 degrees, 42 minutes, 51 seconds, north.

[22] See my work, *The Secrets of Nostradamus*, 2001, pp. 81–83. Nostradamus gave the precise dates using astrological coordinates.

[23] In quatrain II.24, Nostradamus used the word *Hister*. Both Hitler and Goebbels were in no doubt that this was a reference to the Fuhrer himself. See Ellic Howe, *Nostradamus and the Nazis, A Footnote to the History of the Third Reich*, privately printed, with no date, op. cit., n.xi, above. My own view is that Nostradamus was referring to the river Danube, which in Roman times was called the *Hister*.

[24] For Franco, see quatrain IX.16. I have dealt with this in my work, *The Secrets of Nostradamus*, 2001. For General de Gaulle, see quatrain I.50. I have dealt with this in op. cit., pp. 87–97 (esp. 96).

[25] It was founded in 1764, as a fur-trading post, by Pierre Laclède.

[26] About 1986, a copy of a book on astrology, by the important Arabic astrologer Al-Kabisi, was discovered in the Municipal Library, Lyons. The title page contained the autographic ex-libris of Nostradamus, along with the price he paid for it, and the date of purchase—1560.

This work was purchased by Nostradamus after he had published the *Prophéties*; otherwise it would have been of profound interest to us in the present context because of its extensive choreographies, or tabulation of planetary and sign rulerships over places. The first part of the work, *Liber introductorius*, contains far more than a representation of astrological techniques, for it includes a number of lists of climata, and place names, with their zodiacal and planetary influences.

[27] This phrase occurs, for example, in quatrain I.55.

[28] This is in quatrain I.24, which I have dealt with in *The Secrets of Nostradamus*, pp. 291–3.

[29] Whether or not Nostradamus was aware of these three interlinked meanings is questionable, but I have no doubt that he was familiar with the secondary meaning—that is, within the Latin *fatulus*. He was both a Latin and Greek scholar.

[30] Actually, following the tradition behind such code-making, it could have been coded as follows:

esPARSE SAutera = PARSESA with one transmutation permitted = PASERA

[31] The Parsees were Zoroastrian fire worshippers, originally from Persia. To avoid Muslim persecutions, in the eighth century, they fled to India.

[32] See quatrain X.21: it is a reference to Persia because Nostradamus refers, in the same line, to the Magi (*les Magues*), who were reputed to have come from this country. In the *Gospel of St. Matthew*, 2:1, the Magi are merely recorded has having come "from the east," following the star.

[33] This is quatrain III.64.

[34] See William Smith, *Dictionary of Greek and Roman Geography*, 1870, Vol. I, pp. 982–3, and Vol II, p. 555.

[35] The two works of Arrian that deal with this part of the world, the *Anabasis* and the *Indica*, had been published in 1535 by Trancavalius. In his *Indica*, Arrian uses the word *Cophen* for Kabul (a name applied to the river as well as the province.) A good modern bilingual edition is by P.A. Brunt, *Arrian with an English Translation*, Vol. II, 1983.

[36] For example, in the excellent dictionary of Larive and Fleury, *Dictionnaire Francais Illustré des Mots et des Choses . . .* , 1903, the word *Normans* is defined as (and I translate): "Danish and Scandinavian pirates, who, in the ninth to the 10th century, invaded and devastated France, England, Germany and Friseland. . . . One of their chiefs, Rollon, obtained from Charles the Simple, by the treaty of Saint-Claire-sur-Epte (912 AD), that part of the Neustrie which, after their own name, is called Normandy."

[37] I have taken this line from the Pierre du Ruau edition. *Caspre* is not found in any French dictionary. Given the context, I presume it is a variant of the rare French word *capre*, which is derived from the Dutch, *kaper*. In the 15th and 16th centuries, this was a name given to a type of ship used by the most feared pirates of the day—the Corsairs, from the northern coasts of Africa.

[38] The five names published by the FBI were Walid Al Shehri, Wail Asheri, Mohammad Atta, Aabdul Alomari and Satam Sugami. The same report, of September 14, 2001, listed for the second airplane the names Marwan Alsshemmi, Fayez Ahmed and Mohald Alshehri. Two others were named as being possibly linked with this

second hijack: Hamza al Ghamdi and Ahmed Al Ghamdi. I have derived this material from news reports.

[39] This is from the 1557 Antoine du Rosne edition of *Les Propheties de M. Michel Nostradamus*, printed in Lyon. It has survived without significant mutilation, into modern times. The most important change—of *Ceucalion* to *Deucalion*—I deal with in the following text.

[40] For example, in quatrain IV.29, which relates to the voyages of discovery undertaken by the English seaman, Captain Cook.

[41] Ovid, *Metamorphoses*, II.215ff.

[42] The word appears in the form *Deucalion* in the 1668 edition, published by Jean Iansson, in Amsterdam. The story of Deucalion may offer signs of being the equivalent, in Greek mythology, of the biblical Noah, but the Greek story is directly derived from the ancient Egyptian flood legends.

[43] The Greek name for this group of stars was Καλπη (*kalpe*), meaning "Urn," or "pitcher." For an example, see the second-century AD astrologer Vettius Valens, in the W. Kroll edition of 1908, 12:29.

[44] Ovid, *Metamorphoses*, l.262ff.

[45] R.H. Allen, *Star-Names and their Meanings*, in the 1963 edn, p. 47. The Arabic name, *Al Dalw*, means the well bucket, and this may also have come directly from the Babylonian.

[46] There are many variant details in the telling of these ancient myths. I have recorded the ones told by Ovid, as these are undoubtedly the ones with which Nostradamus was familiar.

[47] Ovid, *Metamorphoses*, I.386ff.

[48] The proposal, of two and a half centuries, comes from William Smith, *Dictionary of Greek and Roman Geography*, 1870, Vol. II, p. 909.

[49] Eratosthenes certainly included the stars of *Chelae* with those of Scorpius. See, for example, Richard Hinckley Allen, *Star Names. Their Lore and Meaning*, 1963 edn., pp. 269ff.

[50] I suspect that it is intended to link with the Greek λαεργής [*laerges*], meaning "made of stone." Libra, so to speak, dropped him like a stone. The relevance of this suggestion lies in the fact that, in ancient Greece, Libra was called the Στάτηρ [stater], or Weight.

[51] Variations, all of which may be regarded as being valid, do affect the meaning of certain undertones in the quatrain, but not its general thrust. These variations include Rigaud 1566: [l.1: soubz signez] [l.2: multe contre advis:] [l.3: Change perille pence,] and [l.4: le {*pro* se}]. In 1568: [l.1 soulz].

As the above notes indicate, the 1566 edition gives, in the third line, the phrase *en perille pence*. Although I have not adopted this French, I think that it is worth commenting upon its possible meaning: within the framework of the Declaration, it could be construed as meaning "dangerous thought" (*penser* is the verb "to think"), for the revolutionary content of the Declaration was, in its time, a challenge to existing authority.

Garencières (see n. 5 above) had no qualms about reproducing the equivalent of the 1566 version, and this has overspilled into the modern subcultural Nostradamian literature. In particular, the words *perille pence*, which, as I have said, is the 1668 version of the original *pareille trense*, has misled both Henry C. Roberts and Erika Cheetham, the leaders of the subcultural school. Cheetham, thinking that the quatrain might apply to Francis II, speculates that Nostradamus might have known some English (which, as a matter of fact, he did), and suggests that the word applies to English coinage. She makes no attempt to explain what the quatrain would mean, given this curious interpretation. Roberts, who records the same Garencières version, is equally out of his depth, in interpreting the quatrain as a prediction of the Islamic revolution in Iran.

[52] Ebenezer Wild, in his diary for July 4, 1776, recorded that in the evening, "the army turned out & fired a fudey joy to celebrate the Glorious Independence of America." The delightful *fudey joy* is almost Nostradamian, and is *un feu de joie*. See *Massachussetts Historical Society's Proceedings*, 2nd series vi. p. 111.

[53] William H. Michael, *The Declaration of Independence. Illustrated Story of Its Adoption, With the Biographies and Portraits of the Signers and of the Secretary of the Congress*, 1904, p. 6. I call this book "official" because it was published by the Government Printing Office, Washington, D.C.

[54] See Thomas Fleming, *1776: Year of Illusions*, 1975, pp. 277–78. According to Michael, op. cit. n. 53 above, it was signed by 50 members on August 2, Mr. Houston of Georgia being absent on a mission. Whythe signed on or about August 27; Richard Henry Lee, Gerry and Wolcott in September. Thornton signed in November, and McKean, probably in 1781.

[55] The Gregorian calendar was not adopted in France until 1584, 16 years after the death of Nostradamus. It was adopted in Britain, and in consequence, in the American colonies, in 1751.

[56] For example, in Pennsylvania, "the heart of the Union," many cit-

izens refused to swear an oath countermanding their allegiance to the king. The state population was 300,000, yet only 6,000 went to the polls. Fleming, taking into account the voting rights, and "a presumed enthusiasm for independence," estimates that the figure should have been closer to 60,000. See Fleming *op. cit.*, p. 278. For source and futher details, see Allan Nevins, *The American States during and after the Revolution*, 1924, p. 149.

[57] Morris' concern was that it had already caused division among the delegates. See Fleming, op. cit., p. 331. See also Montross, note 58 below, p. 171.

[58] Lynn Montross, *The Reluctant Rebels: The Story of the Continental Congress*, 1950.

[59] Quoted by Henry P. Johnson, *The Campaign of 1776 around New York and Brooklyn*, in *Memoirs of the Long Island Historical Society*, vol. 3 (1878), pp. 216–17. For his record of the reluctance of the state to agree on opposing Britain, see Charles Lee, *The Lee Papers*, 1871, vol. 2, pp. 222–24.

[60] Fleming, op. cit., p. 301. William B. Reed, *The Life and Correspondence of Joseph Reed*, vol. 1, p. 213.

[61] See Douglas S. Freeman, *George Washington: A Biography, 1948–57*, Vol. 4, p. 139, as given by Fleming, op. cit. n. 56 above, pp. 282–3. Ira D. Gruber, *The Howe Brothers and the American Revolution*, 1972, p. 94, offers slightly different words.

[62] Fleming, op. cit., pp. 288–89.

[63] In effect, this reading is based on the 1668 edition, which includes an accent on *aisnée*. Variant readings include 1557: [l.1: La saeur aisnee {ae in ligature, and no accent in aisnee} l'isle], [l.2: devat naissance:], [l.4: balance.].

[64] A fine example, which does not stray beyond the prophecies made by Nostradamus, is the imposing statue to the Admiral Coligny, in front of the Temple de l'Oratoire, Paris. The personification of France is female, just as is the personification of Religion. In my 1966 edition of Henry C. Roberts' inane *The Complete Prophecies of Nostradamus*, p. 143 are some anonymous pencillings which insist that the Republic of France cannot be a brother, since it is *feminine always*. The same anonymous writer links Great Britain with John Bull, the mythological collective Englishman, which may have been invented by John Arbuthnot, in *Law is a Bottomless Pit*, 1712. While I take this anonymous writer's point, I still think that the argument

I assemble for the notion of a masculine France, in this context of the Revolution, is a valid one.

[65] See Louis Gottschalk & Margaret Maddox, *Lafayette in the French Revolution. From the October Days through the Federation*, 1973, p. 290.

[66] This bronze stands at the western side of the Place des États-Unis, laid out in 1866. The other statue of Washington is in the Place d'Idéna. This was designed by David French and Edward Potter for the women of the United States of America, and given to France in recognition of the help given by this nation to America during the War of Independence.

[67] *Dr. Brewer's History of France*, 1896, p. 306

[68] From the notes left by Nostradamus, in his *Epistle to Henri II*, we may have no doubt that he took the dates for the Planetary Ages directly from the Latin text of Trithemius, *De Septem Secundadeis*, 1520.

[69] See Rodney Collin, *The Theory of Celestial Influence. Man, the Universe and Cosmic Mystery*, 1971 edition. The theory is neatly summarized in Appendix Eight, pp. 361–367.

[70] I have adopted the reading from 1668 edition, which does not introduce the abbreviations. In doing this, I have ignored the capitalizations introduced by the editor of 1668. The edition variations are obvious: 1557: [l.1: Enuosigee] [l.2: cité neufue:] [l.3: grās lōg tēs ferōt]. 1558: [l.1: Ennosigee] [l.2: cité neuue] [l.3: grāds têps] [l.4: Arethuse nouueau fleuue.].

[71] The Greek epithet for Poseidon as the "earth-shaker," is Ἐωωοοίναισσ' (*Ennosigaios*).

[72] *Mercure de France*, August, 1724. In the facsimile reproduction in *Cahiers Michel Nostradamus*, No.1 March, 1983, p. 9, col. 3.

[73] See Erika Cheetham, *The Prophcies of Nostradamus*, 1973 edn., p. 67.

[74] This is a free rendering of Ovid, *Metamorphoses*, XIII, l. 723–28.

[75] For a long time, I attempted deciphering the quatrain with the notion that the two rocks were reference to the Two Sicilies, which combined Sicily with the mainland of Italy, south of the Papal States. It was not until Sicily was captured by Garibaldi that it was annexed to United Italy in 1860, and the Two Sicilies ceased to exist. However, the events in both Sicily and Naples during the long lifetime of the Two Sicilies did not measure up to the catastrophe of 1943.

[76] See this epithet, and for details of the taking of Pantelleria, see John Terraine, *The Right of the Line. The Royal Air Force in the European War 1939–1945*, 1985, pp. 567–569.

[77] Norman Gelb, *Ike & Monty. Generals at War*, 1994, p. 241.

[78] From a Memorandum of May 1941, written by Trenchard, p. 264, quoted verbatim by Terraine, op. cit. n. 76 above, p. 579.

[79] See W.J. Paul and A.F. Simpson (USAF Historical Division), *The Army Air Forces in World War II. 1965 impression*, (pp. 336ff and 371-407).

[80] G.A. Shepperd, *The Italian Campaign, 1939–45*, 1968, p. 22.

[81] Ovid, *Metamorphoses*, V, l. 569ff.

[82] For Nostradamus in Italy, between 1548 and 1549, see Edgar Leroy, *Nostradamus. Ses origines, Sa vie. Son oeuvre*, 1993 edn., pp. 69ff.

[83] See Richard Woodman, *Malta Convoys 1940–1943*, 2000. For the torpedo strike, see pp. 459–60.

[84] Usually, Roberts merely copied his French version of the quatrain, and the corresponding English version, from the 17th-century English translation of Garencières (see n. 5 above). In this case, he seems to have tripped up. For reasons that are not very clear, he recorded a French version of the quatrain which had nothing to do with the Garencières version, yet used Garencière's translation! The fact is that Garencières had copied his own French version from an extremely bowdlerized edition.

[85] Quatrain from 1557. Variants include: 1558: [l.1: Pour gent loingtaine,] [l.2: troublee:] [l.3: different] [l.4: chef, riblee.] 1568 [l.1: Pour gent estrange, et de Romains loingtaine,] [l.2: troublee:] [l.3: Fille sans main different] [l.4: chef, riblee.] 1668: [l.1: & de Romains loingtaine,] l.2: eau] [l.3: Fille sans main, different] [l.4: chef].

[86] *Ribler* is a specialist verb, usually restricted to milling, and to stone-work (perhaps derived from ribbing the millstone). How this might be linked with the idea of metal-working may be adduced from the fact that the French noun *riblons* means "scrap iron."

[87] A wall was built, shortly after 1900, to prevent further land erosion on the riverside. For an account of the early town, see L.G. Tyler, *The Cradle of the Republic: Jamestown and James River*, 1906 [2nd edn].

[88] *The Epistle of Paul the Apostle to the Romans*, 2:14.

[89] Quatrain from 1557. Edition variants include: 1558: [l.1: l'on verra] [l.2: tendants:] [l.3: l'on orra,] [l.4: feu faim, mort les attendants.], 1650: [l.2: tendans:] [l.4: faim mort les attendans.], 1668: [l.2: tendans:] [l.4: faim mort les attendans.].

[90] From the notes left by Nostradamus, in his Epistle to Henri II, we may have no doubt that he took the date for the Planetary Ages directly from Trithemius, *De Septem Secundadeis*, 1520.

[91] The engraving is a detail from the section "De Causa Meteororum Efficiente," in Robert Fludd's *Philosophia sacra et vere Christiana Seu Meteorologia Cosmica*, 1626.

[92] For example, in quatrain II:46, he leaves no doubt as to what he has in mind when he offers the line, *Au ciel fer, courant longue estincelle* (Fire in heaven, running a long burning form). In quatrain II:43 he calls the comet *l'estoille chevelue*, the hairy star; and in II:70, he refers to it as *le dard du ciel*, the sky-dart.

[93] Besides Encke's comet, there was a bright (unnamed or unidentified) comet visible in the southern hemisphere in May, and in London from June 22, 1881; Schaeberle's comet was visible from August 26, 1881, and Denning's comet was visible from October 4, 1881. Esotericists would be inclined to claim that this preponderance of comets was itself linked with the change of rulership from Gabriel to Michael, which became effective in that year.

[94] Another comet, first visible in the southern hemisphere, stretched through the skies from early in September 1882. This also was sufficiently bright to be seen in daylight. The comet was drawn by the artist T.E. Key as it was seen from Streatham, at 4:00 A.M., on November 4 of that year.

[95] Ptolemy, who influenced the entire medieval period of astrology (including Nostradamus) set out the rules governing the effects of comets in *Tetrabiblos* II.9. He does not set out the specific influence of Gemini, but he gives the rules by which this influence may be inferred. These specific influences were drawn up by a large number of astrologers who practiced in the medieval period. The general rule is that they produce the effects of the combined Mars and Mercury, which encourage war and "disturbed conditions." In the paragraphs dealing with the comets, Ptolemy states the rule that the peculiar effects of these influences will be directed in terms of the parts of the zodiac in which the head of the comet first appears.

[96] According to R.H. Allen, *Star-Names and their Meanings*, 1963

edn., p. 316, the nebula was not mentioned by Galileo, and it is generally thought to have been discovered by Cysatus of Lucerne, in 1618.

[97] The words of Polymestor, in Euripides, *Hecuba*—the two lines are quoted by Allen, op. cit., p. 304, but it is evident that Euripides had in mind not the star Sirius, but its constellation. Accordingly, I have adjusted the two lines, so that the reference is to constellations, rather than to a combination of constellation and star.

[98] This is in quatrain II:41, which predicts the great *nova* of 1572. The third line reads, "The huge mastiff will howl all night" (*Le gros mastin toute nuict hurlera*). For an analysis, see David Ovason, op. cit., p. 204–8.

[99] It would be tiresome of me to give literary sources for all these historical events. In order to make it easy for the reader to check my assertions, I have used above only material that may be found in standard chronological reference works: for example, in Benjamin Vincent, *Haydn's Dictionary of Dates*, 1885 edn., Neville Williams, *Chronology of the Modern World. 1763 to the present time*, 1966 edn., and L.C. Pascoe (ed.) *Encyclopaedia of Dates and Events*, 1974 edn.

[100] I base this interpretation on the fact that one of the meanings of *rond* is "a sphere" (the *"trois corps ronds"* are the cylinder, the cone and the sphere).

[101] By March 1880, £141,562 had been received from the distress fund. In July 1880, a further £177,401 was received. This was in addition to the charities bestowed from the Commonwealth and the United States.

[102] This seems to have been the original version in which Nostradamus constructed the quatrain (but see the qualifications I set out on page 80). It was certainly repeated in the 1557 edition. However, zealous editors soon "corrected" this Spanish back into French. This kind of editing has been the undoing of Nostradamus.

[103] Ptolemy, *Tetrabiblos*, II, 9.

[104] As an example of an astrologer pointing to such comet-induced events, we may take Alfred John Pearce, *The Text-Book of Astrology*, 1911 edn. pp. 337–347.

[105] See S.F. Baird, *Report of the Board of Regents of the Smithsonian Institution*, 1883, p. 213. For further background on the comet and Garfield, and, indeed, on Trithemian dating, see David Ovason, *The Secret Architecture of Our Nation's Capital*, 2000, esp. Chapter Two, pp. 12–39.

[106] Cornelius Gemma, *Cyclognomica*, 1569, Book II, 1, p. 28. The prophecy mentioned by Gemma involved the occurrence of a sudden highly destructive wind: I take this to be the quatrain for June 1562, in Nostradamus' *Almanach Nouveau* for 1562, dedicated to Pius IV. For the series of monthly prophecies for this year, see R. Benazra, *Répertoire Chronologique Nostradamique (1545–1989)*, 1990, pp. 48–50. Gemma mentions the astrologer (*Mathematicus*) and his *Prognostico*, and dates it for 1562 (*Quidam in suo Prognostico, ante annos octo*). Gemma is far from kind to the astrologer, and suggests that the prediction was lucky (*sed fuit in praedicendo felicior quam speravat*). There is every reason to believe that Nostradamus' contemporaries were under the impression that the Seer based his annual predictions on astrological calculations. According to Gemma, the astrologer had been dead for some time by 1569 (*crederent ut ipso nunc etiam à multis hinc annis vita defuncto*)— Nostradamus had been dead for 3 years. Even so, annual predictions made in his name were still being published (. . . *nomen tamen praedictiones annuae servent*). This is also true of Nostradamus. Even if my proposition, that Gemma is referring to Nostradamus, is incorrect, this in no way diminishes the validity of the prediction for April 1562.

[107] For example, the *Almanach* for 1570 (published in 1569), while recognizing that Nostradamus was *deffunct* (that is, dead), took his name in vain by claiming that it was composed by his disciple, Florent de Crox. Another writer to take on the fame, if not the mantle, of Nostradamus was Antoine Crespin. See 1570, in Benazra, op. cit., pp. 94–97. For Michel Nostradamus *le jeune*, see 1571 (ibid, pp. 97–9). There were to be several 16th-century impostors, and even today, with all the techniques available to bibliographers, the sorting out of the genuine Nostradamus quatrains from the forgeries can be a difficult business.

[108] This was the *Almanach Nouveau, Pour l'An. 1562*, published in Paris by Guillaume le Noire, and Iehans Bonfons.

[109] See Cornelius Gemma, *De Arte Cyclognomica*, 1569, II I, p. 28. As Thorndike [VI 100] points out, Gemma's *a multis hinc annis* cannot be accurate, given his previous "eight years."

[110] The verse is in the *Almanach Nouveau* for 1562, fol. A3r. I have not had an opportunity to examine this almanac: I have taken the quatrain from Robert Benazra's reliable and scholarly work, *Répertoire Chronologique Nostradamique (1545–1989)*, 1990, p. 49.

[111] The names of the ships are not known, but one was 160 tons, and the other 60. On board were 150 volunteers. The ships had set sail from Havre de Grace in February 1562. See Stefan Lorant (ed.), *The New World. The First Pictures of America made by John White and Jacques le Moyne and Engraved by Theodore de Bry*, 1946, p. 6.

[112] Jean Ribault, *The Whole & True Discouerye of Terra Florida*, 1563. I have adapted the fuller quotation given in Lorant, op. cit., n. 114, p. 7.

[113] The publication of Theodor de Bry's *Grands et petits voyages* began in 1598, and took 45 years to complete.

[114] This consisted of three ships, with three hunded men and four women. It was under the command of René de Laudonnière, who had been Ribault's former lieutenant on the first voyage. This more extensive expedition plays no part in the Nostradamus quatrain.

[115] I have taken this verse from the excellent Amsterdam edition of 1668. The readings derived from earlier editions differ so slightly from this that I shall not trouble to record variants individually. Common among the variants are *fleux* for *flux*, and *Angelicque* for *Anglicque*. Both these variants are found in the Pierre Rigaud edition of 1558.

[116] *Whitehall Evening Post*, August 7, 1766: quoted by O.A. Sherrard, *Lord Chatham and America*, 1958, p. 220. Chapter 15 in this work, entitled "That Peerage," is well worth reading in the context of the reception of Pitt's elevation.

[117] By the end of the Seven Years War, Britain had gained not only Canada, but also Nova Scotia, Cape Breton, Florida, Senegal, and the islands of St. Vincent, Tobago, Dominica and Grenada.

[118] The italics are mine. The King's speech was delivered on November 13, 1759—see O.A. Sherrard, *Lord Chatham. Pitt and the Seven Years' War*, 1955, p. 346. The same author, in *Lord Chatham and America*, 1958, p. 356, records Pitt's own equivalent blood imagery, in regard to his fears that war will break out in America. His speech on January 20, 1775 predicted that "the first drop of blood shed in civil and unnatural war" (that is, war with the colonies) would result in a blood wound that could not be quenched. Pitt was a friend of Benjamin Franklin, and was especially well informed of the resentment then being formed against the British government in the Americas. Both men were Masons.

[119] See O.A. Sherrard, *Lord Chatham. Pitt and the Seven Years' War*, 1955, p. 13.

120 I quote from a speech delivered by Pitt on May 26, 1774. For a synopsis of the speech, see O.A. Sherrard, *Lord Chatham and America*, 1958, pp. 348–49.

121 In a speech delivered on January 20, 1775, he argued for the withdrawal of British troops from Boston, on the grounds that "the first drop of blood shed in civil and unnatural war might be *immedicabile vulnus*"—an untreatable wound. See Sherrard, 1958, op cit., p. 356.

122 *Isaiah*, 26:19.

123 This was the translation offered by Garencières (op. cit., n. 5), and, inevitably, it was the one adopted by many modern writers who seem to have had little grasp of the French language. For example, Henry C. Roberts, *The Complete Prophecies of Nostradamus*, 1982 edn, translates *souche* as "log," Erika Cheetham, *The Prophecies of Nostradamus*, 1973 edn, translates it as "stump," and John Hogue, *The Complete Prophecies*, 1997, gives it as "stump of wood." This demonstrates, once again, just how pernicious has been the influence of Garencières.

124 Quatrain is from 1557. Variant quatrains include: 1558: [l.1: foudre or & argent] [l.2: De deux captifs mangera]. 1668: [l.1: foudre or & argent fondu.] [l.2: captifs] [l.4: submergée].

125 I quote from Thomas Fleming, *1776. Year of Illusions*, 1975, p. 339.

126 As a matter of fact, Bushnell had foreseen that the hull might have been sheathed in copper, and had designed the screw system accordingly. Unfortunately, Lee tried to screw into an iron connector linking the rudder hinge with the stern. The operation failed because Lee did not realize that all he had to do was move a few inches. See the letter from Bushnell, in *Transactions of the American Philosophical Society*, 4, 1799, p. 310.

127 It is from the title page of *Les Significations de l'Eclipse, qui fera le 16 September, 1559 . . . par maistre Michel Nostradamus, docteur en medecine de Salon de Craux en Provence*. There is no date of publication, but one presumes that the publisher, Guillaume le Noir, brought it out in 1558. For details, see Robert Benazra, *Répertoire Chronologique Nostradamique (1545–1989)*, 1990, pp. 30–31.

128 The engraving, by Balthazar Schwan, is from Johann Daniel Mylius, *Philosophia Reformata*, 1622.

129 The data, between 1700 and 2050, derived from Michelsen, op. cit., n. 136, p. 34, is as follows:

May 21, 1845	lunar eclipse	0 SAG 21
May 21, 1864	lunar eclipse	0 SAG 34
Nov 23, 1946	solar eclipse	0 SAG 50
Nov 23, 1965	solar eclipse	0 SAG 40
Nov 22, 1984	solar eclipse	0 SAG 50

[130] In fact, the idea was so well established in ancient times that the lunar dragon responsible for this cannibalism had a name. It was called *Atalia*. See Roger Beck, "Interpreting the Ponza Zodiac: I," pp. 9–10, in *Journal of Mithraic Studies*, Vol. 1, No. 1, 1976.

[131] In modern astrology, the meaning has been (wrongly) extended to cover not only this conjunctive yoking, but also the extreme separation of the aspect of opposition.

[132] This language of encoding is now called the *Green Language*. For an account of it, in relation to Nostradamus, see my work, *The Secrets of Nostradamus*, pp. 129ff.

[133] The quatrain is from 1557. Textual variations include: 1558 [l.1: loing defaut grands luminaires.) [l.2: l'Avril] [l.3: cherré!]. 1568: [l.3: cherté!]. 1668: [l.1: loing defaut grands] [l.2: Mars,] [cherté! grands debonnaires,] [l.4: parts.]. I did consider using 1668 for the sample, if only because the exclamation mark that terminates *O quel cherte!* makes more sense of the third line. However, the rhyme of *Mars* with *parts,* in this latter verse, is awkward, and so I preserved the 1557 version, for all its deficiencies.

[134] He used the term *defaut*, or *default*, as the equivalent of eclipse in a number of quatrains. As a matter of fact, he had used the term in the preceding verse to the one I am examining—quatrain III.4.

[135] Garencières, translating the Nostradamus verses into English in 1668, had no doubt that the Master had an eclipse in mind: he rendered the line:

Near the eclipse of the two great luminaries

Unfortunately, Garencières had no knowledge of the Trithemian system that Nostradamus used, even though a poor attempt at an English translation of the Secundadeians had already been published by the astrologer William Lilly in English, and both the Latin and German versions of *De Septem Secundadaeis* were well known to scholars.

[136] The solar eclipses were on January 11, in 22° Capricorn, July 7 in 16° Cancer, December 2 in 11° Sagittarius, and December 31 in 11° Capricorn. I have abstracted this data from Neil. F. Michelsen, *Tables of Planetary Phenomena*, 1993 edn.

[137] The French verb *secourir* is conjugated like the verb *courir*, which means to run. It is also used for a sailing ship, meaning "to sail." The word is derived from the Latin *cucurri*, "to hasten," and [figuratively] "to fly."

[138] The word *cherré* appeared in the 1558 Pierre Rigaud edition, printed in Lyon. It had become *cherte* in the 1568 Benoist Rigaud edition, printed in the same city.

[139] The quatrain is from the Amsterdam 1668 edition. 1605 gives the following variants: [l.1: Au revolu], [l.2: d'Hecatombe:].

[140] Nostradamus seems to have taken the word *revolution* from the astrological literature, for it was not a word used by Trithemius himself, in regard to the cycles of the planetary angels. In the 13th century, Michael Scot certainly used the word *revolution*, and he knew of the Trithemian angels, even though he called them Rectors. Al-Kabisi, whose work Nostradamus purchased in 1560, also used the word *revolution*, in its astrological sense. For details of this work, see *Cahiers M. Nostradamus*, 1986. However, it is only in conjunction with *De Septem Secundadeis* that whole sections of Nostradamus' important letter to Henri II may be understood. Although I give the sources for the term *revolution* and for the parallels Nostradamus draws with *De Septem Secundadeis*, it must be understood that these sections have been constructed by Nostradamus in code. This is understandable, given the interest shown by the recently established Roman Inquisition in such things as prediction.

[141] The word is derived from the Greek, Εκατον, "hundred," and βομς, "oxen." Even by Homeric times, the word was not restricted specifically to the slaughter of a hundred oxen. Nostradamus used the word in several of his quatrains.

[142] *Les batailles modernes sont de véritables hécatombes.* Modern battles are veritable hecatombes. Quoted in Larive et Fleury, *Dictionnaire Francais Illustré des Mots et des Choses*, 1903, Vol. I, p. 944.

[143] According to Gardiner, the earliest full moon in the month of *Apollonios* (of the Elean calendar) fell on August 6, the latest fell on September 5. The earliest full moon in *Parthenios*, of the even Olympiads, fell on August 20, the latest on September 19, and, in two out of the three years it fell between the August 20 and the September 5. For details relating to the most widely accepted of these speculative dates, see N. Gardiner, *Olympia. Its History & Remains*, 1925, pp. 68–73.

[144] This is the spectrum of dating proposed by C.F. Unger, who be-

lieves that the event fell on the second full moon after the summer solstice, and thus between the last days of July and August. See 'Der Olympien monat,' in *Philologus* 33 [1874], pp. 227–28. For dissident views, see J.G. Frazer, *Pausanias's Description of Greece*, 1898, v.9.3.

[145] After 472 BC, the games lasted for five days, on the first and last day of which were staged animal sacrifices. The games were abolished by Theodosius in 393 AD, and revived by Baron Pierre de Cubertin, in Athens, in 1896.

[146] See for example, *The Gospel According to St. John*, 5:28–29, and *The Gospel According to St. Matthew*, 27:51–52.

[147] The portal with three openings, depicted on the coinage of Antonius Pius, Commodus and Marcus Aurelius, is reproduced by J. G. Frazer, in *Pausanias 1898, Commentaries*, Bk. II, iii [p. 23]. He reproduces an example of a Corinthian copper coin of the Imperial period with the Sun god driving his four-horse chariot, ibid, p. 25.

[148] The quatrain is from the Amsterdam 1668 edition. 1605 gives the following variants: [l.1: Au revolu], [l.2: d'Hecatombe:].

[149] Porphyry, *On the Cave of the Nymphs*, in the wonderful Thomas Taylor translation. Needless to say, the Greek and Latin versions of *De Antro* were available in 16th-century France.

[150] One observes also that while the "people" are plural (the verb *sortiront* is third person plural, meaning "they come out), the tomb from which they exit is singular (*tombe*). Again, it is not usual for a group of people to share the same tomb.

[151] One of the technical terms used in space flight is *shroud*. The planned docking of the craft Gemini 9a, in June 1966, is reported to have been aborted because the shroud that covered the docking collar failed to separate.

[152] The Greek and Latin versions of St. John give the word in the plural μνημείοις, in Greek, and *monumentis*, in Latin.

[153] I have abstracted this data from Sybil P. Parker (ed.), *McGraw-Hill Concise Encyclopedia of Science and Technology*, 3rd edn., 1994, p. 1746ff.

[154] See article by Peter Conradi in the World News section of *The Sunday Times*, March 18, 2001, p. 24. The remains of the Mir finally ditched in the Pacific on March 23, 2001 (GMT).

[155] For instance, in quatrain III.46 (which deals with the mysterious city of Plaucus) he mentions the fixed stars in general—*estoilles fixes*. In quatrain II.90, he mentions in particular the two important

stars in the constellation of the Twins (Gemini), Castor and Pollux (actually, *Castor & Polux*), symbols of mortality and immortality, respectively.

[156] See Robert Amadou, *L'Astrologie de Nostradamus. Dossier*. 1992.

[157] Sirius is in 14.07 degrees of Cancer. The MC, or midheaven, at the moment of the first impact was 16 degrees of Cancer.

[158] The lovers were Zulamith the Bold and Salami the Fair. For this Finnish story, see R.H. Allen, op. cit. n. 45, p. 122. In fact, the essay on Sirius in this work (pp. 120–29) is filled with useful mythological imagery, and forms essential supportive reading.